The Church: A Proper Jewish Bride

An Eternal Relationship with Jesus

By: Leigh

Copyright owned by
Leigh Morton
2010
All Rights Reserved

Bread of Life Christian Fellowship
Attention: Sister Leigh
PO Box 20009
Mound House, NV 89721

The right of reproduction of this book is reserved exclusively for the author who grants permission for brief quotes as long as full credit is given to the author. Passages may be quoted in part or in its entirety only by prior written approval of the author.

"Thou shalt not muzzle the ox that treadeth out the corn. And the labourer is worthy of his reward." I Tim 5:18 (I Cor 9:9, Deut 24:15 KJV

"Therefore, behold, I am against the prophets, saith the Lord, that steal my words every one from his neighbor." Jer 23:30 KJV

"…Thou shalt not steal, … Thou shalt love thy neighbor as thyself." Rom 13:9, (Matt 19:18, Mark 10:19, Luke 18:20, I Cor 6:8,10, Eph 4:28, ex 20:15, Lev 19:11, 13, 18, Matt 5:43, 7:12, 19:19, 22:39, Mark 12:31, Gal 5:14, James 2:8) KJV

"Render therefore to all their dues: … honor to whom honor." Rom 13:7 "That no man go beyond and defraud his brother in any matter: because that the lord is the avenger of all such, as we also have forwarded you and testified." I Thes 4:6 (Lev 19:13, Deut 32:35, Prov 22:22, 23) KJV Scriptures complied by the Bluedorns, Triviumpursuit.com

All Bible passages quoted herein are from the New International Version 1984, unless otherwise noted.

ISBN 978-0-9794612-4-8

Dedication:

I give thanks and praise to Jesus, the author and finisher of my faith, for the lessons he has taught me in studying for this book. I have truly become His bride for all eternity!

I want to thank my parents, Dave and Nancy Morton, who tried to instill in each of their children the belief that we could accomplish anything we put our minds to. Without their training I could never have accomplished any of the things that I have done since I have turned my life over to Jesus and started it anew in Him and with Him.

I also want to thank my Pastors, John and Betty Wiltse, for the encouragement they have given me and the discipline they have inspired and instilled in me from the day I first met them.

I wish to give thanks to a couple of my favorite Christian authors and historians, Brock and Bodie Thoene; whose historical Christian novels I have read and enjoyed for many years. And without whom this book wouldn't have been complete. For it was while I was re-reading their series, The AD Chronicles, that I found the scene for the wedding of Joseph and Mary – Jesus' parents. This wedding scene intrigued me. So I have chosen to use this real couple in a fictional setting as a physical, human, example of our relationship with Jesus, our heavenly bridegroom.

Lastly, I would like to thank my sister, Jerri, who graciously allowed me to use her wedding picture as a representation of the Bride of Christ.

Table Of Contents

GOD'S FIRST CHOSEN 10
INTRODUCTION 10
WALKING THROUGH THE STEPS 15
TOWARD OUR SPIRITUAL WEDDING FEAST 15
SELECTION OF THE BRIDE...17
STEP ONE 17
JOSEPH'S BRIDE IS CHOSEN 17
CHRIST'S BRIDE IS CHOSEN 20
PRICE OF THE BRIDE [MOHAR] 22
STEP TWO 22
MARY'S BRIDE PRICE IS SET 23
THE PRICE OF CHRIST'S BRIDE 24
THE FATHER SETS THE PRICE OF CHRIST'S BRIDE......................25
JESUS DESCRIBES HIS BRIDE 26
THE SHEEP AND THE GOATS 39
BETROTHAL [ERUSIN] AND KETUBAH [MARRIAGE CONTRACT]...49
STEP THREE 49
THE TERMS OF MARY'S KETUBAH ARE SET 50
CHRIST PREPARES OUR KETUBAH 52
OUR KETUBAH 52
THE BRIDE'S CONSENT 55
STEP FOUR 55
MARY ACCEPTS HER KETUBAH.....................................56
JESUS PRESENTS OUR KETUBAH TO THE DISCIPLES 57
THE DISCIPLES ACCEPTED OUR KETUBAH 57
THE CUP OF THE COVENANT 58
STEP FIVE 58
MARY DRINKS THE CUP OF THE COVENANT 58
JESUS PASSES THE CUP OF OUR MARRIAGE COVENANT...............60

GIFTS FOR THE BRIDE [MATTAN] 62
STEP SIX 62
MARY RECEIVES BRIDAL GIFTS 62
THE CHURCH RECEIVES GIFTS FROM JESUS 64

THE MIKVAH 67
STEP SEVEN 67
MARY GOES TO THE MIKVAH 67
CHRIST'S BRIDE GOES TO THE MIKVAH 70

DEPARTURE OF THE GROOM 72
STEP EIGHT 72
JOSEPH DEPARTS 72
JESUS PREPARES HIS DISCIPLES THEN DEPARTS 74

THE CONSECRATED BRIDE 78
STEP NINE 78
MARY IS VEILED 78
CHRIST'S BRIDE IS VEILED 79

LESSONS FROM THE TEN VIRGINS 82

RETURN OF THE BRIDEGROOM 96
STEP TEN 96
JOSEPH RETURNS FOR MARY 96
CHRIST IS RETURNING FOR HIS BRIDE 98

THE HUPPAH 99
STEP ELEVEN 99
JOSEPH AND MARY ENTER THEIR BRIDAL CHAMBER 100
THE CHURCH WILL SHARE THE HUPPAH WITH JESUS 101

THE FINAL STEP - THE MARRIAGE SUPPER 102
STEP TWELVE 102
JACOB INVITES HIS GUESTS TO THE FEAST 102
THE MARRIAGE SUPPER OF THE LAMB 104

IN CONCLUSION 107
KISSED BY THE BELOVED 109
OTHER TITLES BY LEIGH 112
OTHER ENDEAVORS BY LEIGH: 112

God's First Chosen
Introduction

The Bible tells us the nation of Israel was Gods chosen people. He made a blood covenant with them and it was sealed by their circumcision[1]; a physical depiction of the blood covenant that Jesus would later consummate on the Cross. He gave them their marriage contract, which was sealed with the blood of their sacrifices, when He handed down the Law on Mount Sinai after releasing them from their bondage in Egypt.

> *Moses then wrote down everything the LORD had said. He got up early the next morning and built an altar at the foot of the mountain and set up twelve stone pillars representing the twelve tribes of Israel. Then he sent young Israelite men, and they offered burnt offerings and sacrificed young bulls as fellowship offerings to the LORD. Moses took half of the blood and put it in bowls, and the other half he sprinkled on the altar. Then he took the Book of the Covenant and read it to the people. They responded, "We will do everything the LORD has said; we will obey." Moses then took the blood, sprinkled it on the people and said, "This is the blood of the covenant that the LORD has made with you in accordance with all these words."*
> **Exodus 24:4-8**

Israel accepted their marriage contract in Exodus 24:3; *When Moses went and told the people all the LORD's words and laws, they responded with one voice,* <u>*"Everything the LORD has said we will do."*</u>

But Israel's relationship with God was a very rocky relationship from the very beginning. This is shown by example in the life of Hosea and his wife Gomer. God told him to '... *Go, take to yourself an adulterous wife and children of unfaithfulness, because the land is guilty of the vilest adultery in departing from the LORD.* **Hosea 1:2b.**

---
[1] **Genesis 17:1-23**

Hosea's marriage was a physical example of Israel's relationship with God from the very beginning. It is 'Reader's Digest Condensed Version,' so to speak. So God divorced Israel. Jeremiah tells us this in 2:1-3a, 2:32-3:2 and 3: 7-8a:

> *The word of the LORD came to me: "Go and proclaim in the hearing of Jerusalem: I remember the devotion of your youth, how as a bride you loved me and followed me through the desert, through a land not sown. Israel was holy to the LORD, the firstfruits of his harvest . . .*

> *You of this generation, consider the word of the LORD …Does a maiden forget her jewelry, a bride her wedding ornaments? Yet my people have forgotten me, days without number. How skilled you are at pursuing love! Even the worst of women can learn from your ways. On your clothes men find the lifeblood of the innocent poor, though you did not catch them breaking in. Yet in spite of all this you say, 'I am innocent; he is not angry with me.' But I will pass judgment on you because you say, 'I have not sinned.' Why do you go about so much, changing your ways? You will be disappointed by Egypt as you were by Assyria. You will also leave that place with your hands on your head, for the LORD has rejected those you trust; you will not be helped by them. "If a man divorces his wife and she leaves him and marries another man, should he return to her again? Would not the land be completely defiled? But you have lived as a prostitute with many lovers— would you now return to me?" declares the LORD. "Look up to the barren heights and see. Is there any place where you have not been ravished? By the roadside you sat waiting for lovers, sat like a nomad in the desert. You have defiled the land with your prostitution and wickedness."*

> *I thought that after she had done all this she would return to me but she did not, and her unfaithful sister Judah saw it. I gave faithless Israel her certificate of divorce and sent her away because of all her adulteries. …*

God knew modern divorce laws before they were ever written. Typically the Petitioner [person wanting the divorce] files the Petition for Dissolution of Marriage. A Summons is issued to the other party with a form to fill out giving their Response. When there is no Response and/or spouses have not made any agreements the Petitioner files the Request to Enter Default. The judge enters the Declaration for Default or Uncontested Dissolution and finally the Judgment.

In the Jeremiah passages above God made His intensions known by filing "His <u>Petition</u> for Dissolution of Marriage." He had legal grounds for divorcing Israel; namely Idolatry and Spiritual Adultery. He <u>Summoned</u> Israel to repentance many times through out the Bible; I found more than 20 times from the book of Jeremiah through the book of Mark. The final Summons' given was made by Jesus in Mark 1:14, 15; *After John was put in prison, Jesus went into Galilee, proclaiming the good news of God. "The time has come," he said. "The kingdom of God is near. Repent and believe the good news!"*

But the nation of Israel didn't fall on her knees and beg God for forgiveness. They failed to <u>Respond</u>. So God filed the <u>Request to Enter Default</u> and sealed His decision while Christ was still on the cross and the temple veil was ripped in two from the top to the bottom[2]. God passed judgment on Israel, His wife. The final Judgment was delivered in AD 70 when the temple of God, the very house where He dwelt with Israel, His wife, was utterly destroyed by the armies of Rome under Tiberius.

After God filed for divorce against the Nation of Israel, He <u>still</u> accepted the repentance of individual Israelites and added those souls to His 'church,' which is His kingdom family and Christ's chosen bride. The Nation of Israel was no longer God's 'chosen people.' Now only those who are a part of His church can be called <u>the Israel of God</u>.

May I never boast except in the cross of our Lord Jesus Christ, through which the world has been crucified to me, and I to the

---

[2] Luke 23:44-46

world. Neither circumcision nor uncircumcision means anything; what counts is a new creation. Peace and mercy to all who follow this rule, <u>even to the Israel of God.</u> Galatians 6:14-16

God knew this was going to happen from the very beginning. He had a plan of redemption and Salvation for men before the earth was created. This plan is Jesus. Now men can choose to accept Him and become His bride.

In I Peter 2:9 KJV, God says of the church; '*But ye are a chosen generation, a <u>royal priesthood</u>, <u>an holy nation</u>, a <u>peculiar people</u>; that ye should shew forth the praises of him who hath called you out of darkness into his marvelous light.*' He took these titles right out of the Old Testament, from Deuteronomy 14:2, KJV it says, *For thou art <u>an holy people</u> unto the LORD thy God, and the LORD hath chosen thee to be a <u>peculiar people</u> unto himself, above all the nations that are upon the earth.* In Exodus 19:6 KJV, God says, *And ye shall be unto me <u>a kingdom of priests,</u> and an <u>holy nation</u> . . .* These titles now fall to every believer and all followers of Jesus Christ, for we were betrothed to Christ when we became believers.

Walk with me as I show you the reflections of *His Church as a Proper Jewish Bride*. Together we will go through the twelve steps of becoming a Jewish Bride and see how we – His church – ARE a Proper Jewish Bride – The Bride of Christ!

Walking Through The Steps Toward Our Spiritual Wedding Feast

Selection Of The Bride
Step One

In ancient Israel, the father of the bridegroom usually chose his bride. In some cases he may send His most trusted servant [if he had servants] to select a bride for his son. We see an example of the father sending his servant in Genesis 24 when Abraham sent his "chief" servant to find a wife for Isaac.

> *Abraham was now old and well advanced in years, and the LORD had blessed him in every way. He said to the chief servant in his household, the one in charge of all that he had, "Put your hand under my thigh. I want you to swear by the LORD, the God of heaven and the God of earth, that you will not get a wife for my son from the daughters of the Canaanites, among whom I am living, but will go to my country and my own relatives and get a wife for my son Isaac."* Genesis 24:1-4

I have written a fictionalization of Joseph and Mary's story. This I have done to bring clarity to the process for becoming married in ancient times and according to Jewish tradition. I know it won't conform exactly to scriptural accounts, for I have taken it from that context into the format necessary to give you the proper perspective to the church as Christ's Bride. I hope you will understand and just see the message of being a proper Jewish Bride.

Joseph's Bride Is Chosen

Joseph and Mary grew up in the same small village on the Galil; the town of Nazareth. They drank water from the same well. Their mothers' bought food from the same venders in the local bazaar. And their families worshiped together in the town's synagogue.

Joseph met Mary when they were children as they romped together in the meadows with the flocks. He a boy of 10 or 12 and she a young lady of 6 or 8; together they kept the sheep and goats of their father's safe from harm with slingshots and smooth stones from the nearby brook. Now they are grown and Joseph is a strong man working in his father's the carpentry shop. Mary, a very beautiful lady, has learned to be a woman at her mother's side. She can preformed all of the household tasks and she knows the arts of making a house into a true home, just like every young lady of her age living in Israel from ancient days to today.

Today is the day that Mary is proclaimed a woman by the priest of their synagogue. Her parents took her to the synagogue and presented her there, as was the custom, to proclaim that she is now of a marriageable age and that would be seeking a proper husband for her. Her father will choose the man who will become her husband. He will be a man of honor, who knows the law and the prophets; a man with a trade who can provide for her and for the children the Almighty will bless them with.

The sun has started to set, and Joseph's mother has dinner on the table for her family. She has asked Joseph to call his father to the table. Joseph has gone to his father's shop to call him for dinner.

"Father, Father?" Joseph yells to Jacob. "Father have you spoken to Heli yet? I am afraid that if you wait much longer some other man will choose her for his son to marry. She is just recently of marriageable age and very beautiful. Heli won't wait long for you to make a decision."

"Joseph," Jacob replied. "Good things come to those who wait. As the Psalmist said; 'Be still before the LORD and wait patiently for him; do not fret when men succeed in their ways, when they carry out their wicked schemes.' If God has chosen her for your wife, it will happen."

All the prominent men of the village meet at the gates in the evenings to discuss important matters. After dinner Jacob goes out to the gates of the village to meet with the men of the town. Heli, Mary's father, is there and he calls Heli aside for a chat. "Heli your daughter, Mary, has caught the eye of my son, Joseph." Jacob begins, "He has asked to marry her. Can we meet to discuss the joining of our family's with their union?"

Heli answers, "Jacob, many suitors are seeking my Mary's hand. What does Joseph offer? Come tomorrow and we will talk about the terms you would propose for this marriage. My wife and I will consider them. If they are acceptable, I will present them to Mary to see if she would be agreeable to this union before I will make a decision on this matter."

"When shall I come?" Jacob asks.

"We shall break the bread of the evening meal together, you and I." Heli replied. "And after we sup, we will retire to my study to discuss your proposal."

These two fathers meet for dinner at the appointed time and spoke together for several hours afterward, discussing the future of their children and the uniting of their families. Even before they came to an agreement both knew that their children loved one another and were well suited to be joined together. While this was not a requirement for a good marriage it would make a good marriage into a great one from very early on. Heli was agreeable to the terms that Jacob ben Judah proposed. He shared the terms of this proposal with his wife and then with his daughter, Mary. All were in agreement with the terms presented. The <u>Choice</u> was made.

Christ's Bride is Chosen

We as Christ's Bride were also chosen. John 15:16 reads; *Jesus said, you did not choose me, but I chose you and appointed you to go and bear fruit—fruit that will last. Then the Father will give you whatever you ask in my name . . . if you belonged to the world, it would love you as its own. As it is, you do not belong to the world, but I have chosen you out of the world. That is why the world hates you.*

If the Lord had not cut short those days, no one would survive. But for the sake of the elect, whom he has chosen, he has shortened them. **Mark 13:20**

In my former book, Theophilus, I wrote about all that Jesus began to do and to teach until the day he was taken up to heaven, after giving instructions through the Holy Spirit to the apostles he had chosen. After his suffering, he showed himself to these men and gave many convincing proofs that he was alive. He appeared to them over a period of forty days and spoke about the kingdom of God. **Acts 1:1-3**

<u>I have written a fictionalization of the choosing of Christ's Bride – The Church – and most of the other steps, too. Please remember that these examples are truly works fiction and come from my imagination, NOT God's Word. But I feel they may be valuable to us as we walk through the steps together. Please understand that I am in no way giving credence to the teachings on the Trinity because I have portrayed Jesus and God, the Father as separate persons – it is just for clarity of the fictionalizing I have done so. I do not agree with those who believe in three person –trinitarian – godhead. But I do not deny that they are Christians. We just have differences in beliefs, which will not keep us from heaven.</u>

"Father," Jesus called. "I have found a beautiful Bride that I would like to bring home to live in our house forever. She is in need of my protection; I love and I must have her – to bring her up into the grace and truth of what <u>real love</u> is."

"Son," GOD replies, "What would you use to purchase this bride, for all brides are rare and precious creatures and worth more than the most valuable rubies I have created."

"My Father," He answers, "I will give my very life if I can but claim this precious PEARL as my very own. For I am the merchant that has been seeking goodly pearls. And I have found the most valuable PEARL of all.[3] I know she isn't much to look at right now, for she is covered with mud and dirt. But I know when we are wed she will shine forth in all MY Glory. I will even give my very life to redeem her, provide for her, love her and call her My very own."

"Son, My heart is with you in this choice of a Bride." GOD agreed, "She is of your heart already and I am please with your decision. She was My Choice for you from the very beginning. I will send you to her to prepare her for a life everlasting in Our Home."

And thus Jesus came to earth as a child, to love and walk among His chosen Bride. To teach her and prepare her for life everlasting!

---

[3] See Matthew 13:44 – 46; for we are Jesus' Pearl of Greatest Price.

Price of the Bride [Mohar]
Step Two

In Biblical times brides were purchased. The bride price [*mohar*] was paid to the father of the bride, both to compensate him for the loss of a worker and to show him how much the bridegroom valued his bride. The groom would have to raise this money while he was preparing their future home. This bride price was usually equal to at least one year of the groom's wages. In Luke the Greek word "mina" is used. It was worth approximately one hundred denarii (more than three months' wages for the average working man). So a years' wages would have been 3.5 and 4 minae. If we were to look at this by today's standards the average man makes somewhere between $25,000 and $50,000, and this would be the absolute minimum he would have to save to marry the lady of his choice. It was a high price, for brides were to be highly valued and not easily obtained.

Proverbs 31:10-12:
Who can find a virtuous woman? For her price is far above rubies. The heart of her husband doth safely trust in her, so that he shall have no need of spoil. She will do him good and not evil all the days of her life.

Above and beyond the bride price, the bridegroom also gave gifts unto his bride [Mattan]. The Mattan could be as much or more than the mohar. This practice is shown in Genesis 24:52-53; *When Abraham's servant heard what they said, he bowed down to the ground before the LORD. Then the servant brought out gold and silver jewelry and articles of clothing and gave them to Rebekah [Mattan]; he also gave costly gifts [Mohar] to her brother and to her mother.* It is mentioned again in Genesis 34:11-12; *Then Shechem said to Dinah's father and brothers, "Let me find favor in your eyes, and I will give you whatever you ask. Make the price for the bride* [Mohar] *and the gift* [Mattan] *I am to bring as great as you like, and I'll pay whatever you ask me. Only give me the girl as my wife."*

Mary's Bride Price is Set

Heli, and Jacob met together to set the terms of Mary's bridal price.

"Heli, my son Joseph has fallen in love with your daughter, Mary and wants to marry her. He has told me he would have no other. What amount do you feel is proper for her mohar?"

"She is my first born, Jacob. She will not come cheap," Jacob replied. "I need to have 5 minae for her."

Jacob and Heli dickered back and forth for a while. Finally they agreed the price Joseph would pay for Mary would be 4 minae. The fathers broke bread together and shared a bottle of wine, then Jacob returned home to let Joseph have the 'good news.'

Joseph made his living in his father's carpenter's shop. He was a maker of fine furniture, built various buildings and other objects of art and necessity. Joseph would give his father 25% of his income for his keep and would save the rest to pay Mary's bride price. The mohar and mattan would take him 18 to 24 months to save. When the bride price and his gift were saved, Joseph and Jacob would make an appointment to see Heli, Mary's father, to formalize the marriage contract [Ketubah] and betrothal [Erusin].

Joseph built Mary a beautiful olivewood box to keep her Ketubah. He engraved it with beautiful pomegranates and grape vines round the top and sides. On the lid was the scene where Rebekah met Isaac. He sealed the box with olive oil and wrapped it in oilcloth. Then he stored it in a cupboard until his wedding day when he would present it to her. He hopes that Mary will add mementos to it year by year as they travel through life together.

The Price Of Christ's Bride

We, as the bride of Christ, have also been purchased with a price, a very high price — the precious blood of Jesus. He chose to shed iit upon a cross on Calvary's hill. This was the price He paid for us, His bride. He has said that we are worth far more than rubies. Proverbs 31:10-12; *A wife of noble character who can find? She is worth far more than rubies. Her husband has full confidence in her and lacks nothing of value. She brings him good, not harm, all the days of her life.*

We were given the righteousness of Christ at our new birth. We stand full of His grace and glory – in fact, when God looks down on us He sees the image of Jesus in our hearts, not the filthy rags that we had owned before.

1 Peter 1:18,19: *For you know that it was not with perishable things such as silver or gold that you were redeemed from the empty way of life handed down to you from your forefathers, but with the precious blood of Christ, a lamb without blemish or defect.*

Ephesians 1:13-14, KJV: *In whom ye also trusted, after that ye heard the word of truth, the gospel of your salvation: in whom also after that ye believed, ye were sealed with that holy Spirit of promise, which is the earnest of our inheritance until the redemption of the purchased possession, unto the praise of his glory.*

1 Corinthians 7:23 says; *You were bought at a price; do not become slaves of men.*

We belong to Christ. He is our Bridegroom and we are His Bride. He will one day come to claim us as his own and take us to His Father's house.

1 Corinthians 6: 19-20: *Do you not know that your body is a temple of the Holy Spirit, who is in you, whom you have received from God? You are not your own; you were bought at a price. Therefore honor God with your body.*

The Father Sets The Price Of Christ's Bride

Jesus is again talking with His Father. This time they are discussing the price He would pay for His bride [us].

"Son," God starts, "I know Your bride is very special to You. I am in agreement that she should become your wife. The mohar will be a very costly, but she is a very precious gift. You will have to give up everything to have her. Including your very life. Is she worth it to you?"

Jesus answers, "Yes, Father she is worth this, and so much more. I love her! I always have!"

"My One and Only Son," God replies, "the price is set, go and prepare for the day you are to be wed."

I think Isaiah said it best when he said:

For to us a child is born, to us a son is given, and the government will be on his shoulders. And he will be called Wonderful Counselor, Mighty God, Everlasting Father, Prince of Peace. Of the greatness of his government and peace there will be no end. He will reign on David's throne and over his kingdom, establishing and upholding it with justice and righteousness from that time on and forever. The zeal of the LORD Almighty will accomplish this.
Isaiah 9:6-7

Jesus Describes His Bride

... Christ loved the church and gave himself up for her to make her holy, cleansing her by the washing with water through the word, and to present her to himself as a radiant church, without stain or wrinkle or any other blemish, but holy and blameless. [4]

> *One of the seven angels who had the seven bowls full of the seven last plagues came and said to me, "Come, I will show you <u>the bride, the wife of the Lamb</u>." And he carried me away in the Spirit to a mountain great and high, and showed me the Holy City, Jerusalem, coming down out of heaven from God. It shone with the glory of God, and its brilliance was like that of a very precious jewel, like a jasper, clear as crystal. It had a great, high wall with twelve gates, and with twelve angels at the gates. On the gates were written the names of the twelve tribes of Israel. There were three gates on the east, three on the north, three on the south and three on the west. The wall of the city had twelve foundations, and on them were the names of the twelve apostles of the Lamb.*
>
> *The angel who talked with me had a measuring rod of gold to measure the city, its gates and its walls. The city was laid out like a square, as long as it was wide. He measured the city with the rod and found it to be 12,000 stadia in length, and as wide and high as it is long. He measured its wall and it was 144 cubits thick, by man's measurement, which the angel was using. The wall was made of jasper, and the city of pure gold, as pure as glass. The foundations of the city walls were decorated with every kind of precious stone. The first foundation was jasper, the second sapphire, the third chalcedony, the fourth emerald, the fifth sardonyx, the sixth carnelian, the seventh chrysolite, the eighth beryl, the ninth topaz, the tenth chrysoprase, the eleventh jacinth, and the twelfth amethyst. The twelve gates were twelve*

---

[4] Ephesians 5:25b-27

pearls, each gate made of a single pearl. The great street of the city was of pure gold, like transparent glass.

I did not see a temple in the city, because the Lord God Almighty and the Lamb are its temple. The city does not need the sun or the moon to shine on it, for the glory of God gives it light, and the Lamb is its lamp. The nations will walk by its light, and the kings of the earth will bring their splendor into it. On no day will its gates ever be shut, for there will be no night there. The glory and honor of the nations will be brought into it. Nothing impure will ever enter it, nor will anyone who does what is shameful or deceitful, but only those whose names are written in the Lamb's book of life.' [5]

~*~

I know this is a large group of scriptures, so let's break it down. The angel told John that he would show him 'the bride – the wife of the Lamb.' Then he went on to describe a great city, the New Jerusalem coming down out of heaven. It was a walled city with twelve gates; formed like a cube.

The Wall - says that we are Sanctified/Set apart unto the Lord, our heavenly Husband. Built of Jasper - Transparent - all is visible, nothing is hidden from His view.

12 Foundations - had the Names of the Apostles in them. It was they who had been directly taught by Jesus and then taught the early Christians what they had been taught.

The City [the Bride] – was formed of pure gold – it was without any impurities or imperfections. Transparent - all is visible, nothing is hidden from His view. All have been refined as with fire, like pure gold in the refiner's kettles after the slag has been scraped off its surface.

---

[5] Revelation 21:9-27

The foundations were decorated with all kinds of precious jewels, just like a crown. These Precious stones were a symbol of the Twelve Tribes of Israel [more precisely The Law and The Prophets]. For these are the way those of ancient times were taught about Jesus. They were the very same stones that God instructed Moses to put on the ephod for the high priest to wear before the Lord as a representation of the twelve tribes of Israel.

These jewels are also symbolic of the many crowns that are mentioned throughout the Bible that will be rewarded to us at His final coming; when He rewards all for the things we have done and the things the things we have not done. These crowns are: the Incorruptible Crown[6], the Crown of Rejoicing[7], the Crown of Righteousness[8], the Crown of Life[9], the Crown of Glory[10] and Honor[11], the Crowns of Gold[12], the Beautiful Crown[13], the Crown of Loving Kindness[14], the Crown of His Tender Mercies[15], the Crown of Knowledge[16], the Holy Crown[17], and the Royal Crown[18]. He rewards us with these crowns because for our faithfulness and for the acts we do in His name. But we must recall the crown He wore in our place during His last hours on earth; the crown of disgrace that He bore for us – the Crown of Thorns[19].

So the foundations of the Heavenly Bride are the teachings of the Apostles, sprinkled with the teachings of the Law and the Prophets and decorated with the jewels of the many precious crowns that are waiting for us when we meet Jesus at His final

---

[6] 1 Corinthians 9:25
[7] 1 Thessalonians 2:19
[8] Proverbs 16:31, 2 Timothy 4:8
[9] Psalms 103:4, James 1:12, Revelation 2:10
[10] Proverbs 4:9, Proverbs 16:31, Proverbs 17:6, Isaiah 28:5, Isaiah 62:3, Jeremiah 13:18, 1 Peter 5:4
[11] Psalms 8:5 NIV, Hebrews 2:7 NIV, Hebrews 2:9 NIV
[12] Revelation 4:4, Revelations 9:7
[13] Ezekiel 16:12, Ezekiel 23:42
[14] Psalm 103:4
[15] Psalm 103:4
[16] Proverbs 14:18
[17] Exodus 29:6, Exodus 39:30, Leviticus 8:9
[18] Isaiah 62:3
[19] Matthew 27:29, Mark 15:17, John 19:2, John 19:5

return. They are yet to come, but here with us in effigy in the symbolism of our likeness as his bride in His final revelation to the apostle John while on the Isle of Patmos.

12 Gates – Had the names of the 12 tribes of Israel on them. *The twelve gates were twelve pearls, each gate made of a single pearl. The great street of the city was of pure gold, like transparent glass.* Revelation 19:21

Bought with a great price, like the Pearl of Great Price that a man gave all that he owned to possess[20] - We are this [these] Pearl[s]; one Pearl for all the gates. He paid the greatest price to obtain it, His death on the cross.

Each gate in the Old city of Jerusalem had a specific purpose and symbolic meaning, these meanings were all fulfilled in Jesus' life, death and resurrection - he paid it all and fulfilled it all, once and for ALL!

The Twelve Gates of the ancient city of Jerusalem were the Sheep Gate, The Fish Gate, The Old Gate, The Valley Gate, The Dung Gate, The Fountain Gate, The Water Gate, The Horse Gate/King's Gate, The East Gate/Beautiful Gate/Golden Gate, The Ephraim Gate, and The Prison Gate. Here I will share how Jesus fulfills all of these gates in us.

The Sheep Gate – This is the Gate through which the temple sacrifices were brought into the city. Jesus is the perfect lamb that was slain for the sins of the world. I like to believe that on the day He was crucified He was led through this gate on the way to the hill of Golgotha.

He was oppressed, and he was afflicted, yet he opened not his mouth: he is brought as a lamb to the slaughter, and as a sheep before her shearers is dumb, so he openeth not his mouth. Isaiah 53:7

---

[20] Matthew 13:45-47

The next day John saw Jesus coming toward him and said, "Look, the Lamb of God, who takes away the sin of the world! This is the one I meant when I said, "A man who comes after me has surpassed me because he was before me." John 1:29, 30

The Fish Gate - the fish, and other wares for sale, were brought into the market place through this gate. This gate is symbolic of our jobs, careers or occupations and that we should be occupied with the cares of God's Kingdom.

As Jesus was walking beside the Sea of Galilee, he saw two brothers, Simon called Peter and his brother Andrew. They were casting a net into the lake, for they were fishermen. "Come, follow me," Jesus said, "and I will make you fishers of men." At once they left their nets and followed him. [21]

Jesus called these fishermen to become "fishers of men." They were the first of many that He called to this purpose. Jesus recognized that they were employed, and offered them new employment for the Kingdom of God. And yet they still fished.

We, as His followers today, have also been given the occupation of being fishers of men; the compulsion of fishing for the souls of men in order to draw others into His kingdom was and is of greatest importance. For only those who are a part of the Kingdom of God, are the Bride of Christ. He uses us in the areas we are working in when we come to Him, i.e. if a butcher, sell meat and win souls to the glory of God. This is truth, no matter what your usual occupation.

The Old Gate - is said to be representative of the Old Covenant; which is the Covenant God gave to Abraham. This covenant was renewed generation by generation through Him speaking to the Old Testament patriarchs. Many feel that the Old Covenant was the Law that was handed down to Moses. Even so, Jesus fulfilled

---

[21] Matthew 4:18-20

every aspect of the law in His life, death, burial and resurrection.

Do not think that I have come to abolish the Law or the Prophets; I have not come to abolish them but to fulfill them. I tell you the truth, until heaven and earth disappear, not the smallest letter, not the least stroke of a pen, will by any means disappear from the Law until everything is accomplished. **Matthew 5:17, 18**

After this, Jesus knowing that all things were accomplished, that the scripture might be fulfilled, saith, I thirst. Now there was set a vessel full of vinegar: and filled a sponge with vinegar, and put it upon hyssop, and put it into His mouth. When Jesus therefore had received the vinegar, He said, <u>It is finished</u>: and He bowed His head, and gave up the ghost. **John 19:28-30.**

With these final words that were spoken by Jesus, He completed it all. The Law and the Prophets is complete. Hallelujah!

In fact, all that was foretold by the Patriarchs and Prophets was fulfilled while Jesus was here the first time through the things that He said and did, except for one thing – The Feast Of Trumpets. This feast, the last of the Old Testaments celebrations, may also be called the Marriage Supper of The Lamb. It will be fulfilled when Christ returns for His bride.

The Valley Gate – this gate led to the Valley of Hinnom, and the place called Gehenna. Originally it was a place dedicated to the worship of Molech and the burning human sacrifices. Later it was a place where the fires never went out from all of the defiled things, refuse and garbage, which were burnt there. As David implied in His most known Psalm, Valleys in our life are dark places.

I have thought long and hard on these dark places. Mountaintops have nice, scenic views, so they are symbolic of the high times we have in the Spirit. We can look down on the battles just fought and the victories won with rejoicing. But there is little growth going on there on those peaks.

It is in the valleys, in the dark places, that growth takes place. It is also where the mountain streams flow through to nourish the growth on their way to the seas. The living waters of the Holy Spirit strengthen and feed us in our valleys and bring growth in our spirits. And when we pass the test Jesus leads us to the mountaintops once again.

Even though I walk through the valley of the shadow of death, I will fear no evil, for you are with me; your rod and your staff, they comfort me.[22]

Mountaintop experiences are wonderful and very necessary, for our victories are celebrated there. But we <u>all</u> need the valleys, for this is where our growing is done. Accept your valleys, and learn much. Then come to the mountaintops to celebrate your victories with Jesus and other saints who have also triumphed!

The Dung Gate - The way to the trash dump. This is figurative of what our righteousness is in the eyes of God, before Salvation. And how He imputed the righteousness of Jesus to us when we answered His call and came to Him for salvation. We all have to pass through the Dung Gate before coming to the Cross. We must realize that we are sinners and that we need a Savior. We need Jesus to remove the dung and to clothe us in His righteousness.

But we are all as an unclean thing, and all our righteousnesses are as filthy rags; and we all do fade as a leaf; and our iniquities, like the wind, have taken us away. Isaiah 64:6 KJV

I delight greatly in the LORD; my soul rejoices in my God. For he has clothed me with garments of salvation and arrayed me in a robe of righteousness, as a bridegroom adorns his head like a priest, and as a bride adorns herself with her jewels. Isaiah 61:10

What is more, I consider everything a loss compared to the surpassing greatness of knowing Christ Jesus my Lord, for whose

---

[22] Psalms 23:4

sake I have lost all things. I consider them <u>rubbish</u>,[23] that I may gain Christ and be found in him, not having a righteousness of my own that comes from the law, but that which is through faith in Christ—the righteousness that comes from God and is by faith. **Philippians 3:8-9**

Jesus has taken out the trash that once was within the Bride. And He is continuously scrapping off the slag, which mars our surface that reflects His image. Christ's bride has walked through the Dung Gate and left the refuse far behind!

The Fountain Gate – this gate was near the pool of Siloam. It was said to be representative of the Holy Spirit. It may have been built by an artesian well, thus contained "living water." Jesus spoke of giving "living water" to the Samaritan woman at the well:

> *The Samaritan woman said to him, "You are a Jew and I am a Samaritan woman. How can you ask me for a drink?" (For Jews do not associate with Samaritans.)*
>
> *Jesus answered her, "If you knew the gift of God and who it is that asks you for a drink, you would have asked him and he would have given you living water."*
>
> *"Sir," the woman said, "you have nothing to draw with and the well is deep. Where can you get this living water? Are you greater than our father Jacob, who gave us the well and drank from it himself, as did also his sons and his flocks and herds?"*
>
> *Jesus answered, "Everyone who drinks this water will be thirsty again, but whoever drinks the water I give him will never thirst. Indeed, the water I give him will become in him a spring of water welling up to eternal life."*

---

[23] dung

The woman said to him, "Sir, give me this water so that I won't get thirsty and have to keep coming here to draw water."[24]

When we receive Salvation in Christ Jesus, we are given His Holy Spirit to live within us. He leads and guides us in our new life. But there is more of the Spirit of God available to as many as ask for it. Jesus spoke of it in Luke 24:49, KJV:

And, behold, I send the promise of my Father upon you: but tarry ye in the city of Jerusalem, until ye be endued with power from on high.

And the gift was given to men for the first time in Acts 2:1-4: *When the day of Pentecost came, they were all together in one place. Suddenly a sound like the blowing of a violent wind came from heaven and filled the whole house where they were sitting. They saw what seemed to be tongues of fire that separated and came to rest on each of them. All of them were filled with the Holy Spirit and began to speak in other tongues as the Spirit enabled them.*

This fullness of the Holy Spirit is still available for all believers today, seek God with all of your heart, in truth and sincerity, and He will pour it out on you.

Romans 11:29: *... for God's gifts and his call are irrevocable.*

So just believe and receive. Walk through the Fountain Gate to receive the living waters of His Holy Spirit. May they always bubble forth from within you.

The Water Gate - The Gibeonites [water bearers due to their deceit to Joshua and all of Israel][25] brought in the water to be used in the city through this gate.

---

[24] John 4:9-15
[25] Joshua 9

This gate was said to be symbolic of the word of God; of which Paul said in Ephesians 5:25-27; *Husbands, love your wives, just as Christ loved the church and gave himself up for her to make her holy, cleansing her by <u>the washing with water through the word</u>, and to present her to himself as a radiant church, without stain or wrinkle or any other blemish, but holy and blameless.* We know the word of God as the Bible. When this verse was spoken the written word of God was just the Old Testament. But Jesus also spoke God's word while He walked among us. He allowed us to see how to live rightly by His very life. His apostles carried Jesus' words in their hearts and minds, and spoke them again and again through out their ministry. They also carried His example of holy living within them, and did their best to live likewise.

When we study the Bible, it washes our hearts and minds, renewing them and purifying us continually. As long as we follow after God and live according to the example given in His word. This is exactly what Paul was saying to the Ephesians in the passage above. This is what walking through the Water Gate is all about.

The Horse Gate - This was the *King's Gate,* the gate through which His horsemen rode when going to or from battle. In the Old Testament the Israelites were always fighting the enemies that lived around them – the Philistines, Amorites, Ammonites, etc. As Christians we also battle continually. But Paul tells us that ours is not a physical battle like Israel of old fought; no it is a spiritual battle:

For our struggle is not against flesh and blood, but against the rulers, against the authorities, against the powers of this dark world and against the spiritual forces of evil in the heavenly realms.[26]

---

[26] Ephesians 6:12

When we have committed ourselves to Jesus, He becomes our King, and the Battle belongs to the Him. He gave us armor for protection and weapons to defend ourselves with:

> *Finally, be strong in the Lord and in his mighty power. Put on the full armor of God so that you can take your stand against the devil's schemes ... Therefore put on the full armor of God, so that when the day of evil comes, you may be able to stand your ground, and after you have done everything, to stand. Stand firm then, with the belt of truth buckled around your waist, with the breastplate of righteousness in place, and with your feet fitted with the readiness that comes from the gospel of peace. In addition to all this, take up the shield of faith, with which you can extinguish all the flaming arrows of the evil one. Take the helmet of salvation and the sword of the Spirit, which is the word of God. And pray in the Spirit on all occasions with all kinds of prayers and requests. With this in mind, be alert and always keep on praying for all the saints.*[27]

And we never really fight alone. We fight in the power and strength of the Lord God Almighty!

All those gathered here will know that it is not by sword or spear that the LORD saves; for the battle is the LORD's, and he will give all of you into our hands. **1 Samuel 17:47**

> *I saw heaven standing open and there before me was a white horse, whose rider is called Faithful and True. With justice he judges and makes war. His eyes are like blazing fire, and on his head are many crowns. He has a name written on him that no one knows but he himself. He is dressed in a robe dipped in blood, and his name is the Word of God. The armies of heaven were following him, riding on white horses and dressed in fine linen, white and clean. Out of his mouth comes a sharp sword with which to strike down the nations. "He will rule them with an iron scepter.*

---

[27] Ephesians 6:10-11 and 13-18

> *He treads the winepress of the fury of the wrath of God Almighty.*[28]

Praise be to Jesus – He fights beside us, in us and through us!

The East Gate - **Also called the Beautiful or Golden Gate. This is the gate where, it is believed, the Messiah will enter the city of Jerusalem when he returns. It <u>is</u> the gate of our heart that He enters when we make Him King and Lord of our life. It is also symbolic of the gate into our heavenly home.**

Those whom I love I rebuke and discipline. So be earnest, and repent. Here I am! <u>I stand at the door and knock. If anyone hears my voice and opens the door, I will come in and eat with him, and he with me.</u>

To him who overcomes, I will give the right to sit with me on my throne, just as I overcame and sat down with my Father on his throne.[29]

As Christians, as Christ's Bride, we <u>have been</u> seated with Him in heavenly places since the beginning of our relationship with Him. For we have allowed Him entrance into the throne room of our very heart. The heavenly throne is symbolic. It represents the place where Jesus dwells continually; and that place is our inner most being. I know that I have said this before, but it bears repeating here. The place that Jesus went to prepare for us[30] **is not some mystical mansion high in the skies, called heaven; no, it is the rooms of our heart and mind. This is the place He most wants to dwell in, so this is the place He has gone to prepare; to sweep out the cobwebs of our past lives and make totally new. David wanted Jesus to be able to dwell within him when he wrote Psalm 51, for he said:**

Cleanse me with hyssop, and I will be clean; wash me, and I will be whiter than snow. Let me hear joy and gladness; let the bones

---

[28] Revelation 19:11-15
[29] Revelation 3:19-21
[30] John 14:1-3

you have crushed rejoice. Hide your face from my sins and blot out all my iniquity.

Create in me a pure heart, O God, and renew a steadfast spirit within me. Do not cast me from your presence or take your Holy Spirit from me. Restore to me the joy of your salvation and grant me a willing spirit, to sustain me.[31]

When David prayed these things the Holy Spirit didn't live within the hearts of men. He came and went as men's hearts were prepared or not. David had felt the presence of the Holy Spirit many times, but here the Spirit was gone. David had sinned and the Spirit had left him. David had a heart that truly wanted to serve God, so he repented and asked the Lord to let His Spirit return to lead and guide him once more.
Behold the King has entered the East Gate of ALL who have asked Him to rule and reign within them! And yet we still await His ultimate return to earth to carry His Bride away. Come quickly, Lord Jesus, come.

The Miphkad Gate - This is the gate of Inspection and is said to be symbolic of the Great White Throne Judgment. All men, saints and sinners alike, will be judged of God at Christ's return.

But now he [Christ][32] *has appeared once for all at the end of the ages to do away with sin by the sacrifice of himself. Just as man is destined to die once, and after that to face judgment, so Christ was sacrificed once to take away the sins of many people …*
Hebrews 9:26b-28a

So we make it our goal to please him, whether we are at home in the body or away from it. For we must all appear before the judgment seat of Christ, that each one may receive what is due him for the things done while in the body, whether good or bad.
2 Corinthians 5:9-10

---

[31] Psalms 51:7-12
[32] Words in parenthesis added for clarity.

As Paul has said, we must inspect ourselves to see if there be any sin within. For Jesus will inspect us at the final judgment to see if we pass muster, so to speak. He will separate us according to what we have done for Him and His Kingdom, as is recorded in Matthew chapter 25:

The Sheep and the Goats

When the Son of Man comes in his glory, and all the angels with him, he will sit on his throne in heavenly glory. All the nations will be gathered before him, and he will separate the people one from another as a shepherd separates the sheep from the goats. He will put the sheep on his right and the goats on his left.

Then the King will say to those on his right, "Come, you who are blessed by my Father; take your inheritance, the kingdom prepared for you since the creation of the world. For I was hungry and you gave me something to eat, I was thirsty and you gave me something to drink, I was a stranger and you invited me in, I needed clothes and you clothed me, I was sick and you looked after me, I was in prison and you came to visit me."

Then the righteous will answer him, "Lord, when did we see you hungry and feed you, or thirsty and give you something to drink? When did we see you a stranger and invite you in, or needing clothes and clothe you? When did we see you sick or in prison and go to visit you?"

The King will reply, "I tell you the truth, whatever you did for one of the least of these brothers of mine, you did for me."

Then he will say to those on his left, "Depart from me, you who are cursed, into the eternal fire prepared for the devil and his angels. For I was hungry and you gave me nothing to eat, I was thirsty and you gave me nothing to drink, I was a stranger and you did not invite me in, I needed clothes and you did not clothe me, I was sick and in prison and you did not look after me."

They also will answer, "Lord, when did we see you hungry or thirsty or a stranger or needing clothes or sick or in prison, and did not help you?"

He will reply, "I tell you the truth, whatever you did not do for one of the least of these, you did not do for me."

Then they will go away to eternal punishment, but the righteous to eternal life.

Reading through this passage again, I am reminded of the song Keith Green wrote based on it. I have to agree with his findings; the only difference between the sheep and the goats is <u>what they did and did not DO.</u> In fact, it is the very same difference as those between the wise and foolish virgins we discussed just a few pages ago.

Sheep are relatively docile creatures, and Christ likened the church to them on more than one occasion. Sheep are known for following their shepherd. Yes you get a rare one occasionally that tries to go astray, but by and large sheep are followers.

Goats on the other hand are rather stubborn. They prefer to break free from the shepherd when he is leading them to a pasture of sweet, green grass, beside the babbling brook. Their eyes have caught sight of a shiny or interesting object that they MUST go check out. They toss it about and play 'kick the can' with it for a while. Finally when they get tired of it, they toss it one last time and catch it in their mouth to devour it. Later that night when they are trying to sleep that thing they were so fond of earlier in the day has given them indigestion. Go Figure!

People are just like the sheep and the goats. And Jesus will separate us into our respective herds at the final judgment and send us where we belong for all eternity. I am so glad that I have finally decided not to tug against the shepherd's crook, and to be happy to just follow after Him forever.

So, which herd do you think you belong in?

Joshua said to the Israelites long ago, and Jesus repeats the appeal to us today:

But if serving the LORD seems undesirable to you, <u>then choose for yourselves this day whom you will serve</u>, whether the gods your forefathers served beyond the River, or the gods of the Amorites, in whose land you are living. <u>But as for me and my household, we will serve the LORD</u>."[33]

Choose today whom you will truly serve – and prepare for the final judgment of God where we will all walk through the Miphkad Gate to our final, our eternal, destination.

The Ephraim Gate - A Northern Gate looking out over the land of Ephraim [which means doubly fruitful - Jew & Gentile / Earthly & Heavenly]

I will surely bless you and make your descendants as numerous <u>as the stars in the sky</u> and <u>as the sand on the seashore</u>. Your descendants will take possession of the cities of their enemies, and through your offspring all nations on earth will be blessed, because you have obeyed me." **Genesis 22:17-18**

We are the children of the promise God made to Abraham. We are the Israel of God. Paul reminds us of this:[34]

May I never boast except in the cross of our Lord Jesus Christ, through which the world has been crucified to me, and I to the world. Neither circumcision nor uncircumcision means anything; what counts is a new creation. Peace and mercy to all who follow this rule, even to <u>the Israel of God.</u>

As children of the promise to Abraham, we are blessed; and we are blessed again as children of God and joint heirs with Jesus.

The Spirit Himself bears witness with our spirit that we are children of God, and if children, then heirs—heirs of God and

---

[33] Joshua 24:15
[34] Galatians 6:15-16

joint heirs with Christ, if indeed we suffer with Him, that we may also be glorified together. **Romans 8:16-17 NKJV**

It matters not to God whether you are Jew or Gentile, slave or freemen. He has called each of us to be children of the promise, children of God Most High. He has called ALL to receive His double portion; His two fold blessing.

So, as much as in me is, I am ready to preach the gospel to you that are at Rome also. For I am not ashamed of the gospel of Christ: for it is the power of God unto salvation to every one that believeth; to the Jew first, and also to the Greek. For therein is the righteousness of God revealed from faith to faith: as it is written, the just shall live by faith. **Romans 1:15-17**

By accepting Him we show His righteousness to the world. For once we walked in darkness of spirit, but when Jesus comes within, we walk in the light, for He is that very Light!

> *And you will be called priests of the LORD, you will be named ministers of our God. You will feed on the wealth of nations, and in their riches you will boast. <u>Instead of their shame my people will receive a double portion</u>, and instead of disgrace they will rejoice in their inheritance; and <u>so they will inherit a double portion in their land</u>, and everlasting joy will be theirs. "For I, the LORD, love justice; I hate robbery and iniquity. In my faithfulness I will reward them and make an everlasting covenant with them.* **Isaiah 61:6-8**

The Bride walks through the Ephraim Gate and receives a double portion from her Heavenly Bridegroom. Come walk through the gate, be of the bride and be eternally, Doubly Blessed!

The Prison Gate - This is where they held prisoners [the jail]. Peter is seen in Acts 12 being led out of this gate by an angel. Each of us, before we came to Jesus, were in prison to our various sins and vices. He came to set the captives free. He also sets actual prisoners free from their jail cells. I know this personally. I was in a California jail facing a year in prison and a large fine, but Jesus gave me a second chance [or possibly my 100th]. He saw my heart and showed it to the judge who in the Mercy of the Lord set me free after serving only seven days, <u>and</u> without paying any fine.

> *The Spirit of the Sovereign LORD is on me, because the LORD has anointed me to preach good news to the poor. He has sent me to bind up the brokenhearted, to proclaim freedom for the captives and release from darkness for the prisoners, to proclaim the year of the LORD's favor and the day of vengeance of our God, to comfort all who mourn, and provide for those who grieve in Zion— to bestow on them a crown of beauty instead of ashes, the oil of gladness instead of mourning, and a garment of praise instead of a spirit of despair. They will be called oaks of righteousness, a planting of the LORD for the display of his splendor.* **Isaiah 61:1-3**

> *Jesus returned to Galilee in the power of the Spirit, and news about him spread through the whole countryside. He taught in their synagogues, and everyone praised him.*
>
> *He went to Nazareth, where he had been brought up, and on the Sabbath day he went into the synagogue, as was his custom. And he stood up to read. The scroll of the prophet Isaiah was handed to him. Unrolling it, he found the place where it is written:*
>
> *"The Spirit of the Lord is on me, because he has anointed me to preach good news to the poor. He has sent me to proclaim freedom for the prisoners and recovery of sight for the blind, to release the oppressed, to proclaim the year of the Lord's favor."*
>
> *Then he rolled up the scroll, gave it back to the attendant and sat down. The eyes of everyone in the synagogue were fastened on him, and he began by saying to them, "Today*

this scripture is fulfilled in your hearing." Luke 4:14-21

Jesus announced in His home church that He was their Messiah, but they rejected Him. They were in bondage to the traditions and man made laws of the Jewish Religion. Jesus was offering them freedom. They didn't believe or receive what He had to say. They could not accept that He was opening the doors to their own personal prisons. They were bound and blind. The final gate the Bride has walked through is the Prison Gate. She is Free At Last!

While John the Baptist was in Herod's prison he sent his disciples to Jesus to ask if He was the one they sought, or if they were to keep looking. In reply Jesus quoted part of this very passage in Isaiah:

> *When the men came to Jesus, they said, "John the Baptist sent us to you to ask, 'Are you the one who was to come, or should we expect someone else?'"*
>
> *At that very time Jesus cured many who had diseases, sicknesses and evil spirits, and gave sight to many who were blind. So he replied to the messengers, "Go back and report to John what you have seen and heard: The blind receive sight, the lame walk, those who have leprosy are cured, the deaf hear, the dead are raised, and the good news is preached to the poor. Blessed is the man who does not fall away on account of me."* [35]

Jesus came in days of old to set us free from whatever prisons were holding us captive, keeping us from worshiping Him and enjoying His presence in our lives. But there are many who refuse to unstop their ears and open their eyes to the truth of His gospel of peace.

Those of the Bride have walked through the 12 gates in their walk with Him. They are preparing to spend all eternity with Him when He returns. May ALL be so prepared!

---

[35] Luke 7:20-23

The great street of the city was of pure gold, like transparent glass. Rev 21:21b

The street was of pure gold, transparent and clear as glass - the way through the city was clothed with the righteousness of the Holy Spirit. The Holy of Holies is now within the heart of every believer. It is no longer hidden behind the veil of the temple, or the dark recesses of our finite minds. But living and breathing and in full view of <u>all who would behold it.</u> And it is in the heart of the Bride, right where it belongs!

I did not see a temple in the city, because the Lord God Almighty and the Lamb are its temple. Revelation 21: 22

As His Bride, we are the true abode of Jesus. He is our Lord God Almighty. With Him living inside of us, we live and move and have our being truly in Him and Him alone. He is our Life, our very reason for existence. Therefore, there is no longer any place for a physical temple for God to dwell in. For He has been allowed access to the temple He originally created as His dwelling place; the hearts and lives of the men and women He created!

The city does not need the sun or the moon to shine on it, for the glory of God gives it light, and the Lamb is its lamp. Revelation 21:23

This perfect abode of God has no need of any artificial light. It only has need of that Light which comes directly from Him. The lesser lights of sun, moon, and stars pale in comparison to that true illumination which comes for Jesus alone and shines through the lives of His followers. For they have found True Light and no longer does darkness dwell in them or around them in any way. They have truly been given to the Light in every aspect of their being. They have learned the truth of <u>'dio a luz'</u>[36] . . . <u>'given to light!'</u> The Bride has been birthed into THE everlasting Life and Light of Jesus, her Beloved.

On no day will its gates ever be shut, for there will be no night there. **Revelation 21:25**

This new life in His light CAN'T be shut up behind any gate or wall, it shines forth and will make itself known wherever it may be - it can't be hidden under a bushel, or any other barrier. It knows no boundaries. And no darkness or night can abide anywhere close to it. There is no evil that can take up residence within His Light, nor can any sickness or sin. They have all been banished forever!

And the nations of them which are saved shall walk in the light of it: and the kings of the earth do bring their glory and honor into it. **Revelation 21:26**

In this verse He fulfills for eternity His promise to Abraham that all the nations of the earth shall be blessed through his Descendant, his Seed.

> *Christ hath redeemed us from the curse of the law, being made a curse for us: for it is written, Cursed is every one that hangeth on a tree: That the blessing of Abraham might come on the Gentiles through Jesus Christ; that we might receive the promise of the Spirit through faith. Brethren, I speak after the manner of men; though it be but a man's covenant, yet if it be confirmed, no man disannulleth, or addeth thereto. Now to Abraham and his seed were the promises made. He saith not, And to seeds, as of many; but as of one, And to thy seed, which is Christ.*[37]

Nothing impure will ever enter it, nor will anyone who does what is shameful or deceitful, but only those whose names are written in the Lamb's book of life. **Revelation 21:27**

---

[36] This is a Spanish term for childbirth. How appropriate for those who are born again.
[37] Galatians 3:13-16

One who is a true part of Christ's Bride will have no room within them to allow anything in that is not of Him. He is Truth; no lie can enter in. He is Light; no darkness can exist in His presence. He is Holy and Righteous; hatred, deceit, wickedness or anything evil cannot come near to Him or to those that are His. Only those found written in the Lamb's book of Life - the True Believers and Followers - will be a part of His everlasting Kingdom; His Holy and Perfect Bride!

… And as the bridegroom rejoiceth over the bride, so shall thy God rejoice over thee. **Isaiah 62:5b**

And I John saw the holy city, New Jerusalem, coming down from God out of heaven, <u>prepared as a bride adorned for her husband.</u> **Revelation 21:2**

And the Spirit and the bride say, Come. And let him that heareth say, Come. And let him that is athirst come. And whosoever will, let him take the water of life freely. **Revelation 22:17**

Yes we, His Bride, are the heavenly New Jerusalem, the Great and Coming City of Peace, Ruled by the Prince of Peace; Jesus Christ, the King of Kings and Lord of Lords and our Heavenly Husband; Amen.

Even so, Lord Jesus, Come!

Betrothal [Erusin] And Ketubah [Marriage Contract]
Step Three

The ancient Jewish marriage consisted of two main parts. It began with the betrothal [erusin]. The betrothal is much like our engagement today, but it carries a much deeper commitment. It was legally binding and would require a bill of divorce to break. Covenants throughout the ancient world, including those in the Bible, were very serious; and they were final. Sometimes they were sealed in blood, other times with the sharing of a glass of wine, but they were <u>always</u> legally binding. Once a couple entered into the covenant of betrothal [erusin], they were married in all aspects except for the physical consummation of the marriage.

At the betrothal, the marriage contract [Ketubah] was presented to the father of the bride. The Ketubah contained of all the bridegroom's responsibilities and promises to his bride. When given to a woman, she would cherish her Ketubah all of her life.

We have a Ketubah from our heavenly Bridegroom. Our marriage contract is found in God's Word. Our Ketubah is the New Testament. Our marital contract shows us all Jesus gives us as the Bride of Christ. <u>All</u>, not some, of the promises in the New Testament are for us. As His bride, we are fully entitled to them.

> **Jeremiah 31:31-34;** *"The time is coming," declares the LORD, "when I will make a new covenant with the house of Israel and with the house of Judah. It will not be like the covenant I made with their forefathers when I took them by the hand to lead them out of Egypt, because they broke my covenant, though I was a husband to them," declares the LORD. "This is the covenant I will make with the house of Israel after that time," declares the LORD. "I will put my law in their minds and write it on their hearts. I will be their God, and they will be my people. No longer will a man teach his neighbor, or a man his brother, saying, 'Know the*

LORD,' because they will all know me, from the least of them to the greatest," declares the LORD. "For I will forgive their wickedness and will remember their sins no more."

The Terms Of Mary's Ketubah Are Set

Jacob and Joseph are in the home of Heli, Mary's father together with the priest of their of the local synagogue. This meeting is to present Mary's Ketubah, or bridal contract to Heli. The men sit together at meat [or dinner] and are served by the women of the home, including Mary.

"Heli, your wife sets a fine table." Jacob stated, "This rack of lamb is delicious!"

"Thank you, Jacob," Heli replied, "we had an abundance of lambs born this season. They have all been very tender."

After the meal the table is cleared and a scroll is unrolled on it. The men read through it one last time to see that all is set down just as was talked about and that both fathers are in agreement with its conditions.

"Joseph, you have agreed to the bride price of 4 minae." Heli begins, "I know the price is high, but she is my first born and most precious to me."

"Yes Heli, it is high." Joseph agrees, "But Mary is more precious to me than anything in the world. It will take me a while, but I will pay every last mina agreed upon to have my love as my wife."

"So, the mohar[38] has been set," the priest remarks. "Are all in agreement with the terms of the Ketubah?"

"Yes," the men reply in chorus.

---

[38] Mohar = Bride Price

"Joseph, have you decided upon a Mattan[39] to give Mary?" the priest continued.

"Yes, sir." Joseph declared, "I have made her an ornately carved chest. When I present it to her it will contain her Ketubah and a mina. Heli, may I present it to her tonight?

"Is this acceptable to the fathers?" the priest asked

Together the fathers replied, "Yes, the Mohar and Mattan are acceptable."

After the men had agreed to the Ketubah, Mohar and Mattan they filled a glass with wine and passed it around the table, sharing it together.

---

[39] Mattan = Gift for the bride from her husband.

Christ Prepares Our Ketubah

As I stated in detail in the Introduction, Israel [God's first wife] broke her Ketubah with God continually. They had committed adultery with many foreign gods throughout the Old Testament. Even though God hates divorce, He began the divorce of Israel in the book of Jeremiah. Also in Jeremiah God told Israel that He would make a new covenant in the future. He made this new covenant between Jesus and the Church; The New Testament is our Ketubah.

The writer of the book of Hebrews spoke of our marital covenant with Jesus in the following passages to tell them of the new covenant and to remind the Jews of the original covenant with God and how it was broken:

> **Hebrews 8:7-9, 13:** *For if there had been nothing wrong with that first covenant, no place would have been sought for another. But God found fault with the people and said:*
>
> *The time is coming, declares the Lord, when I will make a new covenant with the house of Israel and with the house of Judah. It will not be like the covenant I made with their forefathers when I took them by the hand to lead them out of Egypt, because they did not remain faithful to my covenant, and I turned away from them, declares the Lord …*
>
> *… By calling this covenant "<u>new</u>," he has made the first one obsolete; <u>and what is obsolete</u> and aging <u>will soon disappear.</u>*

Our Ketubah

Jesus and the Father are once again talking; this time they are discussing the terms of our marriage contract.

"Son," The Father begins, "We have decided that you will be giving your life in order to wed the bride you have chosen. This is the mohar we have agreed upon. We must now decide the full terms of the Ketubah."

"Yes, Father," Jesus agrees. "I will give my life for the church. My blood given will wipe away their sin, just as if they had never been committed. It will allow them to live with us evermore."

"Once the price is paid," God continues, "and the world sees you are really dead you will stay in the depths of the earth for three days so there can be no doubts that you were dead. This will honor the terms of the Ketubah. Then my Spirit will enter the depths of the grave and I will bring you out and present you once again to your bride.

"Wonderful, Father! Then I can tell her I am going to prepare a wonder place for us to spend eternity."

"Son have you decided what you will give the church as her mattan?" The Father asks.

"Yes, Father, I have." Jesus answers, "There are many gifts I want to bestow on my Bride. I think when she accepts the Ketubah she should receive a measure of faith and a portion of the Holy Spirit."

"Son, those are great gifts." The Father responds.

"But Father, there is so much more I want to give her." Jesus interjects, "As our relationship grows and matures I have set aside for my church; words of wisdom, messages of knowledge, gifts of great faith, gifts of healing, gifts of miracles, words of prophecy, discerning of spirits, various types of tongues, and the interpretation of those tongues and many more to come!"

"Jesus, You have chosen your gifts very wisely." The Father states, "And I like the way you have chosen to distribute the mattan. Giving gifts throughout the betrothal period, as your relationship grows and matures, is a great blessing to your church and shows your trust in her. It will also help her trust in you to build each day as she awaits your return. I approve both the mohar and the mattan! You may present it to your bride to see if she accepts.

The Bride's Consent
Step Four

Although his father or the father's representative selected a bride for the bridegroom, the woman still had a choice. In Genesis Rebekah was asked, concerning Isaac: *"Will you go with this man?"* **She said,** *"I will go."* **She gave her consent — her "I do."**[40]

God is a gentlemen, He never forces anyone to choose Him. He never takes anyone against his or her will. He calls all to Salvation, inviting each one to be of His Bride. In fact the Bible says that '... *Many are called, but <u>few are chosen</u>.*[41] **I did a little research on this verse and found that it would be better translated '...<u>*few HAVE chosen.*</u>' Few have chosen to be wed to our Heavenly Bridegroom.**

John 3:18-20 KJV says: *Whoever believes in him is not condemned, but whoever does not believe stands condemned already because he has not believed in the name of God's one and only Son. This is the verdict: Light has come into the world, but men loved darkness instead of light because their deeds were evil. Everyone who does evil hates the light, and will not come into the light for fear that his deeds will be exposed.*

This is why so many have not chosen to join His Bride, His church. They do not want to be in the light for it exposes their sin. They would rather continue in their darkness, because it is comfortable – its what they know. And they are afraid of leaving their comfort zones, afraid of the unknown.

When we say, "I do" to Jesus, we must believe in Him with our whole heart and make a verbal confession of this belief. This instruction is given to us in Romans 10:9-10:

That if you confess with your mouth, "Jesus is Lord," and believe in your heart that God raised him from the dead, you will be saved.

---

[40] Genesis 24:57-58
[41] Matthew 22:14

For it is with your heart that you believe and are justified, and it is with your mouth that you confess and are saved.

Have you said your "I do's" to Jesus?

Yes – I do confess that Jesus Christ is Lord.
Yes – I do believe that Jesus died for my sins.
Yes – I do believe in my heart and confess with my mouth that God raised Christ from the dead.
Yes – I do repent of my sins.
Yes – I do give You my heart!
Yes – I do receive Your great love and Your gift of eternal life.
Yes – I will be Your bride forevermore!
Yes – I do say 'I do' to Jesus.

I do! I do! I do!

Mary Accepts Her Ketubah

When all of the discussion was completed by the men folk, Jacob and the priest left Heli's home. Heli called his daughter into the living area. Then he and his wife went into the other room, leaving the couple together to discuss the terms of the proposed Ketubah.

"Mary, I love you very much. I have sat with our fathers and we have come to an agreement on the terms of your proposed Ketubah," Joseph started. "May I read it to you for you to consider its terms and my marriage proposal?"

"Yes, Joseph," Mary replied, "please read the Ketubah."

Joseph read all the terms of their proposed marriage contract then asked, "What do you think, Mary?"

"Joseph, I think it is a wonderful Ketubah." Mary gushes. "I would gladly accept all the terms of it's terms.

Jesus Presents Our Ketubah to the Disciples

Jesus presented our marriage contract when he ate His last Passover feast with His disciples as they were still sitting around the table with Jesus. When they were through eating; *Jesus . . . took bread, gave thanks and broke it, <u>and gave it to them</u>, saying, "This is my body given for you; do this in remembrance of me."* Luke 22:19

This verse was so important that God saw fit to repeat it in three of the four gospels, in fact He repeated it's words twice in the book of Luke – in the passage above and also in Luke 24:30 – when He broke bread with the disciples who had traveled to Emmaus. God always repeats those things that He wants us to pay close attention to. Jesus wanted these disciples to remember when He presented the Ketubah to them so they would get their eyes off their sorrows and back on Him.

The Disciples Accepted Our Ketubah

We can see this clearly in the scriptures, so I don't have to fictionalize it. We read it in the verse quoted above where it says '<u>*and gave it to them*</u>,' If Jesus gave it, then those that received it had accepted it fully and all that the bread stood for. The bread that Jesus broke was His way of presenting our Ketubah to the disciples and they readily accepted it by eating the pieces that were broken.

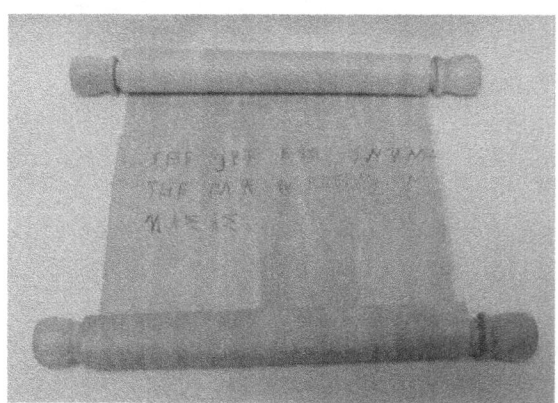

The Cup of the Covenant
Step Five

Before a Betrothal became a valid covenant, the prospective groom would give the proposed bride a cup of wine. He would drink the first sip out of the cup and hand it to her. If she accepted his proposal she would drink the cup of wine down to the very dregs. In doing so she was saying that she was in agreement with all of the terms of the Ketubah and would commit her whole life to carrying out her part.

Most of us would leave the dregs – the sediment - of the wine in the bottom of the cup, as it tends to be very bitter. But when a woman was accepting the marriage proposal of a man she and she was in agreement of the terms of the contract, she would drink this bitter sediment too; to let him know that she would stand beside him no matter what - even through the hard times.

Once the bride's draining of the cup sealed the marriage covenant, the betrothal period began. This period lasted until the groom's father told the groom that it was time to go get his bride. While the bride was waiting, the groom was building and furnishing their new home. Traditionally this was an addition to his fathers' home. This was also the time that he would save up the mohar.'

The bride was also making preparations for their life together. She made garments, blankets, etc for their new home. She also listened closely to all of her mother's, aunts' and grandmothers' words of wisdom about being a wife and mother, keeping them in her heart for that most important day.

Mary Drinks The Cup Of The Covenant
When Joseph finished reading the marriage contract he poured a glass of wine for them.

"Mary," he continued, "will you share the cup of this new covenant with me?"

"Yes, Joseph, I will."

Joseph drank a deep draught from the cup and handed it to Mary. She drank every last drop of that cup of wine. She gave herself to the fullness of her Ketubah with Joseph. This was the beginning of the joining of the houses of Jacob and Heli, sons of David!

Jesus Passes the Cup of Our Marriage Covenant

Again, this was well written of in the word, so I will not make any designs on trying to write it again. Who am I to try to out do God? So I will quote Him here.

Luke 22:14-20 The Message Bible reads:

> *When it was time, he sat down, all the apostles with him, and said, "You've no idea how much I have looked forward to eating this Passover meal with you before I enter my time of suffering. It's the last one I'll eat until we all eat it together in the kingdom of God." Taking the cup, he blessed it, then said, "Take this and pass it among you. As for me, I'll not drink wine again until the kingdom of God arrives." Taking bread, he blessed it, broke it, and gave it to them, saying, "This is my body, given for you. Eat it in my memory." He did the same with the cup after supper, saying, <u>"This cup is the new covenant written in my blood, blood poured out for you.</u>*

As that cup was passed, each of the disciples drank deep; by doing this they were representing the whole of Christ's bride from creation through today and throughout all ages yet to come, until His return. They drained that cup dry. Thus they fulfilled the sharing of the cup of the covenant. In doing so they announced they were willing to follow Him as His bride no matter what the circumstances were – like our modern wedding vows: 'for better or for worse, for richer or poorer, in sickness and in health, till death do us part.' As the Bride of Christ we don't have to worry about death separating us from Him, as stated in Romans 8:38-39:

For I am persuaded, that <u>neither death, nor life, nor angels, nor principalities, nor powers, nor things present, nor things to come, Nor height, nor depth, nor any other creature, shall be able to separate us from the love of God, which is in Christ Jesus our Lord.</u>'

Jesus, just like other Israelite husbands, went back to His father's home to prepare our new dwelling place. He told us His

plans to return in John 14:1-3a, it reads:

"Do not let your hearts be troubled. Trust in God; trust also in me. In my Father's house are many rooms; if it were not so, I would have told you. I am going there to prepare a place for you. And if I go and prepare a place for you, I will come back and take you to be with me that you also may be where I am..."

Gifts for the Bride [Mattan]
Step Six

Every bride enjoys gifts. When they become engaged the groom presents her with a beautiful engagement ring. Then when a couple announces their engagement, friends and family usually throw her a bridal shower. They want to be sure the happy couple have everything they need for their life together.

The Betrothal included the giving of gifts by the bridegroom to his bride. Many times he would give a coin or some other object of value to his betrothed. It would always be something special that would help her remember him while they were apart. The focus of this gift giving was to be on the giver and not on the gift. Today bridegrooms give an engagement ring. This is a symbol of love and commitment. When the bride-to-be looks at her ring, she is reminded of the one who gave her the gift.

Mary Receives Bridal Gifts

After Mary drinks the cup of the covenant Joseph excuses himself and leaves the room. Mary calls her parents back into the room while he is gone. When Joseph returns he has an oilcloth wrapped package in his arms.

Handing the package to Mary, Joseph says; "Heli, I give this gift to your daughter in honor of our marital contract."

"Mary," Joseph continues, "I leave you this gift and my heart until we are joined at the wedding feast."

"Joseph," Mary replies as she opened the cloth, "this box is beautiful. All the intricate engravings are awesome."

"Thank you, Mary. I ask that you do not open the box until we are apart. That way you will have something to remind you of me while we are separated."

"Oh yes, Joseph, that is wise. Thank you again."

"Joseph you have done well this evening," Heli states.

"Heli, I thank you and your wife for honoring my proposal for your daughter in marriage."

The Church Receives Gifts From Jesus

Through Jesus, we, the bride, receive many gifts: Forgiveness, eternal life, fruit of the spirit, the gifts of the spirit, and much more. What bride would say to her bridegroom who comes bearing gifts, "No, I can't accept them"? Yet many of us do that to Jesus, our Bridegroom. Don't miss out on eternity or His precious gifts — decide today to accept all that your Bridegroom has for you.

Don't be deceived, my dear brothers. Every good and perfect gift is from above, coming down from the Father of the heavenly lights, who does not change like shifting shadows. He chose to give us birth through the word of truth, that we might be a kind of firstfruits of all he created. **James 1:16-18**

As His disciples came to believe that Jesus was the promised Messiah, He gave them each a measure of faith. Paul tells us this in Romans.[42] And the writer of the book of Hebrews tells us what this faith is…

Now faith is the substance of things hoped for, the evidence of things not seen. **Hebrews 11:1**

This faith, our 'spiritual engagement ring,' is the promise that Jesus will return just like He said He would. And it lives deep within us just as God had told the Israelites through the prophet Jeremiah;

> *"The time is coming," declares the LORD, "when I will make a new covenant with the house of Israel and with the house of Judah. It will not be like the covenant I made with their forefathers when I took them by the hand to lead them out of Egypt, because they broke my covenant, though I was a husband to them," declares the LORD. "This is the covenant I will make with the house of Israel after that time," declares the LORD. "I will put my law in their minds and write it on their hearts. I will be their God, and they will be my people.* **Jeremiah 31:31-33**

---

[42] Romans 12:3

Before He left earth Jesus also promised His followers that He would send them the gift the Father had promised.

If you love me, you will obey what I command. And I will ask the Father, and he will give you another Counselor to be with you forever— the Spirit of truth. The world cannot accept him, because it neither sees him nor knows him. But you know him, for he lives with you and will be in you. John 14:15-17

On one occasion, while he was eating with them, He gave them this command: *Do not leave Jerusalem, but wait for the gift my Father promised, which you have heard me speak about. For John baptized with water, but in a few days you will be baptized with the Holy Spirit.* Acts 1:4-5

The Holy Spirit doesn't call attention to Himself, but points us to the One who purchased us —Jesus. He also teaches us what we need to know as our relationship with Jesus grows. The book of Psalms is full of places where David and the other Psalmists wrote of being taught of God. Solomon also talked of being taught of 'wisdom' and of listening to the teaching of *'your father.'* How he was sorrowful of not hearing his father's lessons. Yes, he was speaking of his natural father; but the lessons he was speaking of were his father's lessons of God and His ways.

Among all of these I have a favorite:

I will instruct you and teach you in the way you should go; I will counsel you and watch over you. Psalms 32:8

Doesn't this sound exactly like what Jesus was trying to convey in the John 14 passage above?

Christ's gifts are wonderful gifts indeed, but they are only the tip of the ice burg where our heavenly bridegroom is concerned. Throughout the New Testament there are many gifts given to Christ's bride. In Romans 12 it states that prophesy, serving, teaching, encouragement, meeting the needs of others, leadership, and mercy are all spiritual gifts.[43] In 1 Corinthians

12 it speaks of the gifts of wisdom, knowledge, discerning of spirits, faith, working of miracles, different kinds of tongues, interpretation of tongues, and gifts of healing.[44]

Along with these gifts God also 'gives' us the 'fruit of the Spirit.' These are listed in Galatians 5:22-23:

But the fruit of the Spirit is love, joy, peace, patience, kindness, goodness, faithfulness, gentleness and self-control. Against such things there is no law.

Awesome and magnificent gifts our Bridegroom presents to us. Each member of the church has been given his or her own specific gifts and callings. Once the bridegroom has given us His gifts, He will not take them from us, God is no 'Indian Giver.' He tells us so in Romans 11:29: *...for God's gifts and his call are irrevocable.*

But we can throw His gifts away;

> *Furthermore, since <u>they did not think it worthwhile to retain the knowledge of God</u>, he gave them over to a depraved mind, to do what ought not to be done. They have become filled with every kind of wickedness, evil, greed and depravity. They are full of envy, murder, strife, deceit and malice. They are gossips, slanderers, God-haters, insolent, arrogant and boastful; they invent ways of doing evil; they disobey their parents;* **Romans 1:28-30**

There are those, like Judas Iscariot, who feel that having a relationship with Jesus is of little worth. But I will hold on to my bridal gifts from Jesus very tightly, for they are very special to me. Won't you do likewise?

---

[43] Romans 12:6-8
[44] 1 Corinthians 12:4-11

The Mikvah
Step Seven

Brides in ancient Israel, as well as some brides in Israel today, experience a trip to the mikvah prior to her wedding. The word 'mikvah' means 'a pool of living water.' It was used for ritual purification by the Israelites. This immersion and ceremonial washing in water is part of their physical and spiritual preparation for the wedding ceremony. The mikvah represents a separation from the old life to a new life. Figuratively speaking this was a re-birth into her new life as a wife and mother.

Ritual washing wasn't a new thing for the Israelites. Throughout the Old Testament we read of those who were 'unclean' being told to wash and present themselves to the priest as clean in order to participate in their religious practices. There is a great example in Leviticus 14:2 and 8-9, where the Lord told Moses:

> *These are the regulations for the diseased person at the time of his ceremonial cleansing, when he is brought to the priest ... The person to be cleansed must wash his clothes, shave off all his hair and bathe with water; then he will be ceremonially clean. After this he may come into the camp, but he must stay outside his tent for seven days. ⁹ On the seventh day he must shave off all his hair; he must shave his head, his beard, his eyebrows and the rest of his hair. He must wash his clothes and bathe himself with water, and he will be clean.*

Mary Goes to The Mikvah

After hearing of the coming marriage of Joseph and Mary, her friends and sisters gathered at the home of Heli after the evening meal was cleaned up. Giggling through their hand-covered mouths they crept in the back door to sneak Mary out to the local Mikvah.

"Shhh," Mary's sister warns as she grabs some blankets. "Mary is in the barn. We'll go out and get her. She should be done milking the goats by now."

"Ok," the girls whisper as they quietly back out the door they had just entered. It was only a few steps to the barn, so the girls walk there quietly to steal away the unsuspecting Mary.

Upon entering the barn they see Mary wiping her hands on a rag as she leaves the milking stall. "Why are all of you out this late in the evening?" She asks. "The sun is about to set and we should all be going off to bed."

"We're going to the Mikvah," her sister answers. "Its time for you to prepare for your new life."

They all walked down behind the synagogue, toward the local creek. Just beyond the bend in the creek is a quiet cove where the springs run warm, sweet and clear. At the edge of the creek, where the springs pour in, is a pool where the water is warm and deep. This secluded location is the Mikvah, where all the residents of the town come for their ritual washings. Tonight ten young ladies, including Mary's sisters gather to give Mary her premarital cleansing.

Mary enters the pool alone and immerses herself completely. Her sisters and friends then join her and scrub her with pumice-like stones. This scrubbing was symbolic of removing her life prior to marriage. They worked until the top layer of skin was removed and her entire body shone pink in the moonlight. As they finished washing her, they left the pool reciting a prayer while Mary immersed herself again:

"Barukh ata Adonai Eloheynu Melekh Ha-olam asher kid'shanu, be-mitzvotav vitsivanu al ha'tevilah."

When translated into English is: "Praised are you, Adonai, God of all creation, who sanctifies us with your commandments and commanded us concerning immersion."

Their prayer complete, Mary immerses herself once again. Upon rising all of the ladies – Mary included – would recite another prayer:

"Barukh ata Adonai, Eloheynu Melekh Ha-olam sheheheyanu vikiamanu vihigianu lazman hazeh.

Which when translated is: "Blessed are You, Lord our God, Ruler of the Universe, who kept us alive and preserved us and enabled us to reach this season."

Mary would immerse herself one last time, after all the ladies had left the pool and were wrapped in their blankets. Totally alone in the water she makes sure that no part of her body is touching anything else, even another part of her body, until she is totally under the water. She totally immerses herself until all everything, including every inch of her hair, is underwater.

When all is underwater Mary, eyes wide open, curls up into a position like that of a newborn babe. Upon rising she repeats the first prayer once again, but silently; "Barukh ata Adonai Eloheynu Melekh Ha-olam asher kid'shanu, be-mitzvotav vitsivanu al ha'tevilah."

When she has finished her prayers and left the water, her entourage wrapped her in a blanket and dried her off. They redress and quietly walk back into town; each young lady to her own home.

The night is quiet and peaceful. The only sounds heard are the distant noises of the flocks on a nearby hillside. All is at rest and in their places.

Christ's Bride Goes to the Mikvah

In like manner the Bride of Christ also goes to the living waters of the mikvah. When we, as believers in Jesus, are immersed in water baptism, it is our separation from an old life to a new life. Baptism is the outward expression of our new birth in Jesus. It represents the washing, or regeneration, of our spiritual man – our inner most being – our very soul.

When the people heard this, they were cut to the heart and said to Peter and the other apostles, "Brothers, what shall we do?" Peter replied, "Repent and be baptized, every one of you, in the name of Jesus Christ for the forgiveness of your sins. And you will receive the gift of the Holy Spirit. **Acts 2:37-38**

Mark 16:16 reads, *Whoever believes and is baptized* (goes to the mikvah) *will be saved, but whoever does not believe will be condemned.*[45]

Therefore, if anyone is in Christ, he is a new creation; the old has gone, the new has come! **1 Corinthians 5:17**

> *While Apollos was at Corinth, Paul took the road through the interior and arrived at Ephesus. There he found some disciples and asked them, "Did you receive the Holy Spirit when you believed?" They answered, "No, we have not even heard that there is a Holy Spirit." "So Paul asked, "Then what baptism did you receive?" "John's baptism," they replied. Paul said, "John's baptism was a baptism of repentance. He told the people to believe in the one coming after him, that is, in Jesus." On hearing this, they were baptized into the name of the Lord Jesus. When Paul placed his hands on them, the Holy Spirit came on them, and they spoke in tongues and prophesied. There were about twelve men in all.* **Acts 19:1-7**

Most believers are baptized shortly after they have accepted Jesus as their Lord and Savior. They have taken their ritual

---

[45] words in parenthesis added for clarity

bath as a part of Christ's Bride. We do this to let others know that we have taken our relationship with Jesus seriously. We have not only washed ritually, we have also been buried with Him ritually, and raised again to a new life in Him. It is a wonderful beginning to a relationship that will last for all eternally!

Departure of the Groom
Step Eight

Once the marriage covenant was sealed, the bridegroom left his bride and returned to his father's house to prepare a wedding chamber. Before leaving the groom would say to his bride something like, "I am going to prepare a place for you; if I go, I will return to you once again."

He would be gone for twelve months or more. His return was dependant upon his father's approval of the home that he was preparing for his new wife and family. In ancient times it was the custom for the bridegroom to build a home for his new bride as an addition to his father's house. The son would not know when this addition was ready; his father would make that decision. The bridegroom was not allowed to skimp on workmanship or on the materials used, all was to be done 'to code' as it were. Typically it was at least a year – and sometimes two or more years – in the making, but it was not considered ready until his father gave the blessing on their new domicile and released him to fetch his bride.

Joseph Departs

After Joseph has presented Mary with her gifts, he comes to Mary's side and holds out his hand for her to clasp. He tenderly kisses Mary's cheek and kneels before her still holding onto her hand.

"Dearest Mary, I have to leave for now. I am going to prepare a home for you so that we can be together forever. Even though I must leave for a time, I vow I will return at the appointed hour to receive you into my home as you already dwell in my heart."

A single tear forms in Mary's eye as Joseph rises. He raises her hand once more to his lips, kisses it gently and softly says with a choked voice, "Farewell, my love."

Joseph walks to the door of the house. Preparing to exit, he pauses and turns back one last time to get a glimpse of his betrothed, then quietly walks out the door while Mary gently wipes away the tears of joy from her face.

Together they end the evening as Heli recites a passage from the Psalms;

"Where can I go from your Spirit? Where can I flee from your presence? If I go up to the heavens, you are there; if I make my bed in the depths, you are there. If I rise on the wings of the dawn, if I settle on the far side of the sea, even there your hand will guide me, your right hand will hold me fast." [46]

In unison they say, "Amen!" Then the lamps are extinguished as the household retires for the evening.

While there will be no dating or courting – as we know it – by the betrothed couple, Mary and Joseph will see each other from time to time in the normal course of life that exists in their small community. When gathering water from the well, Mary may catch a glimpse of Joseph putting up the walls of their new home or sanding on a piece of furniture. Or when there are services in the synagogue, Joseph may glance up into the woman's area to see his betrothed there – with his mother and her's – listening to the message brought forth by the village priest from God's word. He may even be invited to take a meal with his future in-laws from time to time.

There are many scenarios whereby these two will have a moment to share a bit of time each other during their betrothal period, but it will always be in the company of their family and/or friends. They will never be alone together until he comes for her on the day of their wedding feast.

---

[46] Psalms 139:7-10

Jesus Prepares His Disciples Then Departs

Our Bridegroom, like every other Jewish bridegroom from antiquity, had to leave His bride. Ancient bridegrooms went to prepare a home for the couple to live in. Likewise, Jesus went to prepare an eternal dwelling place for His bride, the church. Throughout His earthly ministry, Jesus made reference to His impending departure. In John 14:1-3, Jesus said:

Do not let your hearts be troubled. Trust in God; trust also in me. In my Father's house are many rooms; if it were not so, I would have told you. I am going there to prepare a place for you. And if I go and prepare a place for you, I will come back and take you to be with me that you also may be where I am.

As I alluded to earlier, the "place" Jesus is preparing for our eternal dwelling is the rooms of our heart; our soul, our very innermost being. He is working, behind the scenes as it were, to sweep out the cobwebs and dispose of all the "skeletons" that we have allowed to enter in and reside there. When He gets one of those "closets" spic and span clean, He fills it up with more of His holy gifts. This allows us to look more and more like Him as time goes by. God wants us to be so clean inside that when we look into our spiritual mirror we don't see our "face." We see His very image shining back at us. He is perfecting us spiritually; bringing us to complete maturity in Christ Jesus. In so much that, not only do we see Him when we look into the mirror, but when others look at us <u>they also</u> see Jesus.

This maturity process takes a while to complete because God isn't just working on one or two people; He is working on the whole church at the very same time. And there are Billions and billions of people that make up the Bride of Christ! This is part of the reason that Jesus tells us that He doesn't know how long He is going to be away. Only the Father of All knows when the place that Jesus is preparing will be completed to His perfection. So Jesus warns His disciples in Mark 13:32-33:

No one knows about that day or hour, not even the angels in heaven, nor the Son, but only the Father. Be on guard! Be alert! You do not know when that time will come.

Just as Jesus was preparing to leave earth to return to His spiritual home He met with His disciples once more. Together they spoke of things to come while He was gone and how to know when His return was eminent. That conversation is in the book of Acts:[47]

> *Until the day he was taken up to heaven, after giving instructions through the Holy Spirit to the apostles he had chosen. After his suffering, he showed himself to these men and gave many convincing proofs that he was alive. He appeared to them over a period of forty days and spoke about the kingdom of God. On one occasion, while he was eating with them, he gave them this command: "Do not leave Jerusalem, but wait for the gift my Father promised, which you have heard me speak about. For John baptized with water, but in a few days you will be baptized with the Holy Spirit." So when they met together, they asked him, "Lord, are you at this time going to restore the kingdom to Israel?" He said to them: "It is not for you to know the times or dates the Father has set by his own authority. But you will receive power when the Holy Spirit comes on you; and you will be my witnesses in Jerusalem, and in all Judea and Samaria, and to the ends of the earth." After he said this, he was taken up before their very eyes, and a cloud hid him from their sight. They were looking intently up into the sky as he was going, when suddenly two men dressed in white stood beside them. "Men of Galilee," they said, "why do you stand here looking into the sky? This same Jesus, who has been taken from you into heaven, will come back in the same way you have seen him go into heaven."*

While we wait for the return of our Bridegroom and King, we need to stay faithful; watchful, focused and spiritually alert. This is the season – the very hour – to pray and fast!

In 1 Peter 4:7 it says; *But the end of all things is at hand; therefore, be serious and watchful in your prayers.*

---

[47] Acts 1:2-11

We should also be doing what we can to get as close to Jesus as we can. Most women preparing to marry try to learn all about their grooms so that they will know how best to make him happy when they are wed. They learn what he likes to eat and how to prepare his favorite meals. What kind of desserts he enjoys, etc. We should also be striving to learn all we can on how to please our Heavenly Bridegroom. I think Paul said it best in 2 Timothy 2:15:

Study to shew thyself approved unto God, a workman that needeth not to be ashamed, rightly dividing the word of truth.

So what should we be studying? God's word, His very thoughts spoken to the various writers and put down on scrolls originally and later transferred into the tomes we now carry around with us or leave on our coffee tables.

We also need to be praying – Prayer is a conversation and must include a time of listening for God to speak to you. He speaks into our hearts and minds with that still small voice which Elijah heard as is recorded in God's word.

Singing songs of worship and thanksgiving can bring you right into His throne room and give you a private audience with Him. The Psalmist tells us to; *"Enter his gates with thanksgiving and his courts with praise; give thanks to him and praise his name."*[48] When we do this, either individually or corporately, we can be moved from our earthly location right into the presence of our heavenly bridegroom. While our praises bring us into His throne room, He also inhabits the praises of His people.

But You are holy, Enthroned in the praises of Israel.[49]

I know that this verse states He inhabits the praises of Israel. But Paul tells us that the church, Christ's bride, is the Israel of God. In his letter to the Christians at Rome he states:

---

[48] Psalms 100:4
[49] Psalm 22:3

It is not as though God's word had failed. For not all who are descended from Israel are Israel. Nor because they are his descendants are they all Abraham's children. On the contrary, "It is through Isaac that your offspring will be reckoned." In other words, it is not the natural children who are God's children, but it is the children of the promise who are regarded as Abraham's offspring. For this was how the promise was stated: "At the appointed time I will return, and Sarah will have a son."
Romans 9:6-9

Paul further said in Galatians 6:14-16:

May I never boast except in the cross of our Lord Jesus Christ, through which the world has been crucified to me, and I to the world. Neither circumcision nor uncircumcision means anything; what counts is a new creation. Peace and mercy to all who follow this rule, even to the Israel of God.

So as Christians, we can be where He is as we lift our songs of praise to Him; and as we praise Him, He will dwell in our praises. This type of contact with Jesus will help us to become closer to Him throughout our betrothal period. The more we offer our praise to Him the more often we will want to do so, so that we can be in His presence. In this way it is like any normal engagement. We prepare for a date with our fiancé, longing to spend as much time with him as possible. We want to be as close to him as we can; longing to know all that we can about him before our wedding. This is normal <u>and expected</u> behavior for both physical and spiritual relationships. Praise Him. Worship Him with your whole being. Spend time with Him and get to know Him. It will serve you well in your relationship with Jesus and the rest of His bride.

As we wait for Jesus, our bridegroom, hold on tightly to His words of assurance:

And if I go and prepare a place for you, I will come back and take you to be with me that you also may be where I am. **John 14:3**

The Consecrated Bride
Step Nine

The Jewish bride was consecrated, set apart, separated unto her bridegroom — the one who purchased her. In this consecration she wore a veil over her face and only removed it in the wedding chamber when at last she was alone with her husband.

Mary Is Veiled

The morning after Joseph leaves Mary's mother brings a new gown and the veil she has made for her daughter's consecration into the family area.

"Mary," she calls. "It is time for the veiling"

Mary's sisters and friends join them in the family area, excited and giggling. They wish Mary well, as her mother dresses her in the new clothes and help her to don her veil. She will remain veiled while in mixed company until the day she is married.

When Mary is dressed her mother says, "Praised are you, Adonai, God of all creation, who sanctifies us. We Thank you for the husband chosen for our precious Mary." Then she turns to her daughter. "Mary, you have been set apart this day to wed Joseph, son of Jacob. May Adonai bless your union with many sons who follow His ways."

"Thank you mother," Mary replied. "and may Adonai bless you and father for permitting me to wed Joseph, son of Jacob. And you, my sisters and friends, may Adonai give you husbands as wonderful as Joseph."

Hugs and tears were shared as the blessings and prayers continued. Mary's mother served bread with butter and honey and warm milk to her family and guests. Then, as it was getting dark, Mary and Heli walk all the ladies to their fathers' homes to assure they are free from harm on the way.

Christ's Bride Is Veiled

As Christ's Bride, we also wear a veil. Paul tells us this in 1Corinthians 13:12; *Now we see but a poor reflection as in a mirror; then we shall see face to face. Now I know in part; then I shall know fully, even as I am fully known.*

Our veil is spiritual, not physical. We don't know all the things we would like to, as God has veiled our minds to keep us pure and safe. This is what Paul was saying in the verse above.

We as Christ's bride are also set apart or sanctified. John 17:18-21 reads: *As you sent me into the world, I have sent them into the world. For them I sanctify myself, that they too may be truly sanctified. "My prayer is not for them alone. I pray also for those who will believe in me through their message, that all of them may be one, Father, just as you are in me and I am in you. May they also be in us so that the world may believe that you have sent me ..."*

Further proof lies in the words of Paul where he said in Acts 20:32, *Now I commit you to God and to the word of his grace, which can build you up and give you an inheritance among all those who are sanctified ...*

God set us apart spiritually when we accepted Him. He will do so in the physical sense When He returns. Jesus prophesied this in Matthew 25:31-33: *When the Son of Man comes in his glory, and all the angels with him, he will sit on his throne in heavenly glory. All the nations will be gathered before him, and he will separate the people one from another as a shepherd separates the sheep from the goats. He will put the sheep on his right and the goats on his left.*

Paul reminds us that: *I have written you quite boldly on some points, as if to remind you of them again, because of the grace God gave me to be a minister of Christ Jesus to the Gentiles with the priestly duty of proclaiming the gospel of God, so that the Gentiles might become an offering acceptable to God, sanctified by the Holy Spirit.* Romans 15:15-16

Do you not know that the wicked will not inherit the kingdom of God? Do not be deceived: Neither the sexually immoral nor idolaters nor adulterers nor male prostitutes nor homosexual offenders nor thieves nor the greedy nor drunkards nor slanderers nor swindlers will inherit the kingdom of God. And that is what some of you were. But you were washed, you were sanctified, you were justified in the name of the Lord Jesus Christ and by the Spirit of our God. **1 Corinthians 6:9-12**

Unto the church of God which is at Corinth, to them that are sanctified in Christ Jesus, called to be saints, with all that in every place call upon the name of Jesus Christ our Lord, both theirs and ours: Grace be unto you, and peace, from God our Father, and from the Lord Jesus Christ. **1 Corinthians 1:2-3 KJV**

While waiting for his return, the bride has to stay faithful. This is easy at first but His return has been long in coming; and it's still ahead of us in 2011. Temptation lies at every hand, and after a while the church may start to give in to it; they may even start to question His return.

2 Peter 3:3-4 reads: *First off, you need to know that in the last days, mockers are going to have a heyday. Reducing everything to the level of their puny feelings, they'll mock, "So what's happened to the promise of his Coming? Our ancestors are dead and buried, and everything's going on just as it has from the first day of creation. Nothing's changed."* **The Message Bible**

We need to stand firm in the power of the Lord. Paul told us of the equipment needed to do so in Ephesians 6:10-18:

> *Finally, be strong in the Lord and in his mighty power. Put on the full armor of God so that you can take your stand against the devil's schemes. For our struggle is not against flesh and blood, but against the rulers, against the authorities, against the powers of this dark world and against the spiritual forces of evil in the heavenly realms. Therefore put on the full armor of God, so that when the day of evil comes, you may be able to stand your ground, and after you have done everything, to stand. Stand firm*

then, with the belt of truth buckled around your waist, with the breastplate of righteousness in place, and with your feet fitted with the readiness that comes from the gospel of peace. In addition to all this, take up the shield of faith, with which you can extinguish all the flaming arrows of the evil one. Take the helmet of salvation and the sword of the Spirit, which is the word of God. And pray in the Spirit on all occasions with all kinds of prayers and requests. With this in mind, be alert and always keep on praying for all the saints.

So, put your armor on. Keep it well oiled and in good repair, and wear it constantly. It will serve you well in fighting off temptations and in the spiritual battles that lie ahead.

Lessons From The Ten Virgins

In this chapter I want to step away from our trip to the altar with Jesus for just a few pages while I share with you the lessons I learned from the Parable of the Ten Virgins in Matthew[50]:

> *At that time the kingdom of heaven will be like ten virgins who took their lamps and went out to meet the bridegroom. Five of them were foolish and five were wise. The foolish ones took their lamps but did not take any oil with them. The wise, however, took oil in jars along with their lamps. The bridegroom was a long time in coming, and they all became drowsy and fell asleep.*
>
> *At midnight the cry rang out: "Here's the bridegroom! Come out to meet him!"*
>
> *Then all the virgins woke up and trimmed their lamps. The foolish ones said to the wise, "Give us some of your oil; our lamps are going out."*
>
> *"No," they replied, "there may not be enough for both us and you. Instead, go to those who sell oil and buy some for yourselves."*
>
> *But while they were on their way to buy the oil, the bridegroom arrived. The virgins who were ready went in with him to the wedding banquet. And the door was shut.*
>
> *Later the others also came. "Sir! Sir!" they said. "Open the door for us!"*
>
> *But he replied, "I tell you the truth, I don't know you."*
>
> *Therefore keep watch, because you do not know the day or the hour.*

---

[50] Matthew 25:1-13

So the Bride of this era in history would call together all of her unmarried [virgin] friends to attend her while waiting for the Bridegroom, and while they were on the way to the wedding feast with the Groom's party and the invited guests, to enjoy the marriage supper after the marriage had been consummated.

They and the Bride would bring their lamps and 'jars' [usually made of clay] with more oil for their lamps. The Bride would have her veil near by and those things she might need during her week of seclusion as well as the gifts the groom had given her before he departed.

As we know the church is the Bride of Christ, John the Baptist tells us this in John 3:28-29, *You yourselves can testify that I said, "I am not the Christ but am sent ahead of him." The bride belongs to the bridegroom. The friend who attends the bridegroom waits and listens for him, and is full of joy when he hears the bridegroom's voice. That joy is mine, and it is now complete.* In this passage John the Baptist claims to be Jesus' best man.

Matthew 9:14-15; *Then John's disciples came and asked him, "How is it that we and the Pharisees fast, but your disciples do not fast?"*
   Jesus answered, "How can the guests of the bridegroom mourn while he is with them? The time will come when the bridegroom will be taken from them; then they will fast ..."

In the Matthew 25 passage Jesus likened the kingdom of God at the time of His return to 10 virgins. The following is what He has taught me about the meaning He had for the parable given above. I will break this down into a verse by verse [more or less] layout to show the things I have learned from Him.

Verse 1-2: *At that time the kingdom of heaven will be like ten virgins who took their lamps and went out to meet the bridegroom. Five of them were foolish and five were wise ...*

Jesus gave the number of virgins as 10. In ancient times 10 was the number of witnesses required in Israel to make a valid quorum.[51] An example of this practice is found in Ruth 4:2-4a:

Boaz took ten of the elders of the town and said, "Sit here," and they did so. Then he said to the kinsman-redeemer, "Naomi, who has come back from Moab, is selling the piece of land that belonged to our brother Elimelech. I thought I should bring the matter to your attention and suggest that you buy it in the presence of these seated here and in the presence of the elders of my people ..."

The virgins in our passage <u>may or may not</u> be saved people. They are those who hang out in Christian circles, like church members and other "religious" people, who are friends or relatives of the Bride. They are there to attend to the Bride and Groom and to light their way to the Marriage Feast.

Verse 3: *The foolish ones took their lamps but did not take any oil with them.*

Jesus said that five of these virgins were wise and five were foolish. The foolish brought no additional oil for their lamps. They made no provision for the future, only brought enough oil for the present. They had not heeded the warning of Solomon in Proverbs 6:6-8:

Go to the ant, you sluggard; consider its ways and be wise! It has no commander, no overseer or ruler, yet it stores its provisions in summer and gathers its food at harvest.

The oil in this parable is representative of several things in scripture, all of which work here. It is representative of the Holy Spirit in our lives, the truth of Christ, the Gospel message and of our salvation. This oil when it is burning and active in our lives causes the Light of His countenance to shine forth through us. We glow from within. So these foolish virgins had made a profession of faith, but they had not filled their hearts with the

---

[51]Definition from www.dictionary.com Quorum: the number of members of a group or organization required to be present to transact business legally, usually a majority.

truth of it's message nor the fullness of its salvation. Their oil would not last long; their light would soon go out. Much like the seed sown on stone ground in Mark:

Others, like seed sown on rocky places, hear the word and at once receive it with joy. But since they have no root, they last only a short time. When trouble or persecution comes because of the word, they quickly fall away.[52]

They had no depth of root so there was no room for them to grow; so they withered up and died.

Verse 4: *The wise, however, took oil in jars along with their lamps.*

The wise virgins had their lamps filled with oil and extra oil in their jars, too. Matthew Henry's commentary states these jars represented their hearts. Not only had they professed their salvation, it was glowing from deep within their inner most beings. They had oil for today and for tomorrow. Their hearts were full and overflowing with His joy.

The wise virgins had provided for the future, yet still Jesus found fault with them <u>and</u> with their foolish friends.

Verse 5: *But while the bridegroom was delayed, they all slumbered and slept.* **NKJV**

The Bridegroom had been long in coming, so the virgins all '<u>slumbered</u>' and '<u>slept</u>.' They were not being watchful for their Bridegroom. They had forgotten their duties as attendants.

In John 14:2-3 Jesus said: *In my Father's house are many rooms; if it were not so, I would have told you. I am going there to prepare a place for you. And if I go and prepare a place for you, I will come back and take you to be with me that you also may be where I am.*

---

[52] Mark 4:16-17

In Matthew 24:36 He also said, *But of that day and hour no one knows, not even the angels of heaven, but My Father only.*

The virgins in this tale had forgotten both of these statements. They left off their duty to be watchful and started to snooze and snore deeply. Jesus planned, and still plans, to return for his bride. But only The Father knows when that return will be. He wants to be sure all is in PERFECT readiness for His Bride before He takes her home to live with Him forever.

I looked up the meaning of the words 'slumbered' and 'slept' in the Strong's concordance to see what the difference was. In the Greek they are two totally different words. The meaning of slumbered is, 'to nod in sleep, to be oppressed with sleep, to be negligent and/or careless. The definition of slept is, 'to fall asleep normally, to yield to sin and/or sloth, to be indifferent to one's salvation, to be dead. I also read In Matthew Henry's Commentary about this passage. He said that the foolish virgins slept, while the wise virgins only slumbered. Looking back at the definitions I felt like Jesus was saying that the wise virgins had gotten <u>negligent</u> in their watchfulness. They were <u>careless about the ways of the Lord</u> and let the focus on their relationship with Jesus slip.

But the foolish virgins were <u>yielded to sloth and sin instead of to Jesus</u>. They were indifferent to salvation and had died spiritually or were very close to death when the bridegroom's cry came.

Verse 6: *And at midnight a cry was heard: 'Behold, the bridegroom is coming; go out to meet him!'*

It seemed to people – both in ancient days and now – that Jesus had taken far too long in His return. Yet God set the perfect time and date for His return. Jesus will never be too early, or too late.
Jesus gave a parable of God's perfect timeline in Luke where He spoke of a certain rich man who had more produce than he

knew what to do with. He decided to build new barns and store his produce for years to come and the Bible says:

> *And he told them this parable: The ground of a certain rich man produced a good crop. He thought to himself, 'What shall I do? I have no place to store my crops.'*
>
> *Then he said, 'This is what I'll do. I will tear down my barns and build bigger ones, and there I will store all my grain and my goods. And I'll say to myself, "You have plenty of good things laid up for many years. Take life easy; eat, drink and be merry."*
>
> *But God said to him, 'You fool! This very night your life will be demanded from you. Then who will get what you have prepared for yourself?'*
>
> *This is how it will be with anyone who stores up things for himself but is not rich toward God.*[53]

The man in this passage had much earthly wealth, but he had nothing with which to honor God. He lost his life because it was God's appointed time for him and he had not prepared for it. And now he was dead. Just like our five unwise virgins.

When Jesus came initially it was kept very quiet. Only a few specifically chosen souls were given admittance to His birth. The second coming of Christ, unlike the first, will be loudly proclaimed. Shouted from the rooftops, so to speak.

1 Corinthians 15:51-52 says: *Listen, I tell you a mystery: We will not all sleep, but we will all be changed— in a flash, in the twinkling of an eye, at the last trumpet. For the trumpet will sound, the dead will be raised imperishable, and we will be changed.*

> 1 Thessalonians 4:15-17 tells us: *According to the Lord's own word, we tell you that we who are still alive, who are*

---

[53] Luke 12:16-21

left till the coming of the Lord, will certainly not precede those who have fallen asleep. For the Lord himself will come down from heaven, with a loud command, with the voice of the archangel and with the trumpet call of God, and the dead in Christ will rise first. After that, we who are still alive and are left will be caught up together with them in the clouds to meet the Lord in the air. And so we will be with the Lord forever. Jesus will clearly announce His return with the shout of the archangel and the sounding of the last trumpet (or shofar). His bride, the church, needs to be prepared.

Verse 7: *Then all the virgins woke up and trimmed their lamps ...*

This verse reminds me of growing up in the country. It seems that just about every year we had heavy storms that would knock out our electricity for days at a time. When we lost power we would have to get all of the kerosene lamps out of the cupboard and prepare them to be used. We would wash the globes, trim the burnt part of the wick back so the unused portion was able to be lit, or replace them if they were too short to burn. Then we would fill the lamps with oil, light the wick, replace the globe and adjust the height of the wick for maximum light and minimum smoking.

With this illustration in mind I can see our virgins waking up at the announcement of the Bridegroom's coming. Blowing out their lamps, trimming their wicks, filling them with oil and relighting them to light the way. These actions symbolize their preparing to meet the Bridegroom when He comes to fetch His bride. These virgins were cutting away the useless things in their lives that had polluted their relationship with Christ, our Bridegroom. They were cleansing their lives from the sins that had caused them to become careless of their Salvation. Refilling their hearts and lives with the oil of His Holy Spirit.

The wise virgins in our parable had taken extra oil in their jars – their hearts. They have recommitted their lives to the Bridegroom. But the foolish do not have any oil left in their lamps, and they didn't bring jars of oil. They had nothing with which to renew their lives. Too late they find they are lacking, their lamps have gone out. They are dead, dead in their spirit; dead unto the Bridegroom, the Lord God.

Verses 8 & 9: *The foolish ones said to the wise, 'Give us some of your oil; our lamps are going out.'*

'No,' they replied, 'there may not be enough for both us and you. Instead, go to those who sell oil and buy some for yourselves.'

These foolish virgins lacked truth in their hearts. They lacked God's grace and Salvation. So, they asked the wise virgins to share the oil they had in their jars. Remember the Strong's definitions sited for the word 'slept' in this parable? Two of these strike me here as I look at the actions of our foolish virgins. First, they were indifferent to Salvation; they gave it little or no thought whatsoever. Second, they were dead in their spirits due to this indifference. I am reminded here of a lesson I learned many years ago; the opposite of LOVE is not hate as many of us believe. Rather it is APATHY. Hate is another emotion reserved for those who have wronged us in some way.

When you love someone you are constantly 'doing' nice things for that person, acts of kindness; gifts for no reason. When you do not love a person you <u>feel nothing</u>, therefore you <u>do nothing</u> for them. This is the state of our foolish virgins; their jars were empty. They felt nothing in their hearts' for our Bridegroom. In their state of apathy, these virgins were selfish. They asked the wise virgins to give up some of their oil. They thought to make further show of their 'faith' while their lights fizzled out and died completely. They sought the comfort of being with those who had the truth without actually <u>having</u> the truth within them. They were fearful of death and darkness. But they didn't want to live the life of the faithful. Instead they sought to die the death thereof. This is why they requested the wise to share their oil with them. In their selfishness they sought to have the grace and the Salvation of the wise, without getting it for themselves.

They also wanted to put the wise in the same position they found themselves in.

But the wise answered, saying, '*Not so; lest there be not enough for us and you: but go ye rather to them that sell, and buy for yourselves.*' Verse 9 KJV

In the original text the two words 'not so' are not there. Translators added them to give clarity to the readers. It was to point out that the wise didn't tell the foolish they wouldn't share their oil straight out; instead they gave a reason why they would not share. <u>Their natural instincts would be to help those in need – always. But they were wise enough to know that giving oil to the foolish would be detrimental to their eternal security, so they declined.</u> They knew that each person needs their own oil of Salvation.

The reply of these wise virgins reminds me of two sayings I have frequently heard within Christian circles, the first being; 'Jesus has no grandchildren.' The second is, 'You can't get to heaven on your parents coattails.' Each person has to have his or her own <u>personal</u> relationship with Jesus – our <u>very own</u> Salvation. The gift of Salvation is actually given to us by Jesus; it doesn't originate within us at all. The wise virgins gave the foolish the very best advice they could: '*Instead, go to those who sell oil and buy some for yourselves.*'

Time had run out on the foolish virgins out for getting their hearts ready for the Bridegroom. He was already in route to the Bride's home to catch her away and take her to His home forevermore. They didn't have time to seek out the truth and be ready when he appeared. Having a jar full of oil is not quickly done. Being full of His Grace, Righteousness and Salvation is a life long process and the wise virgins were prepared when they arrived at the home of the Bride.

Esther gives an example of virgins being prepared for presentation to the King: *Before a girl's turn came to go in to King Xerxes, she had to complete twelve months of beauty treatments prescribed for the women, six months with oil of myrrh and six with perfumes and cosmetics. And this is how she would go to the king: Anything she wanted was given her to take with her from the harem to the king's palace.*[54]

It took much time – at least a year – to be prepared for presentation to their king. In like manner it takes much time for us to be prepared for presentation to our Bridegroom when He returns.

Verse 10; *But while they were on their way to buy the oil, the bridegroom arrived. The virgins who were ready went in with him to the wedding banquet. And the door was shut.*

To keep up appearances, the foolish virgins had to have oil in their lamps in order to go with the bridegroom to the wedding feast. So they left the bride's home to go buy oil in order to <u>look like</u> they were well prepared. When they returned the bridegroom had already come and taken his bride and her attendants, the wise virgins, to the wedding feast. So they went to the bridegroom's home to partake of the wedding feast. The door was shut tight and they couldn't open it. They could not enter the celebration on their own; they had to enter <u>with</u> the bridegroom. So, because these virgins weren't prepared they weren't able to enter and participate with the others.

Hebrews 3:12-15 says; *See to it, brothers, that none of you has a sinful, unbelieving heart that turns away from the living God. But encourage one another daily, as long as it is called Today, so that none of you may be hardened by sin's deceitfulness. We have come to share in Christ if we hold firmly till the end the confidence we had at first. As has just been said:*

"Today, if you hear his voice, do not harden your hearts as you did in the rebellion ,as in the day of trial in the wilderness."[55]

The time for getting right with God is NOW, while it is yet day. For the night is coming then there will be no time left to prepare

---

[54] Esther 2:12-13
[55] Quoted from Psalm 95:7b-8

to enter in. The door will be closed and you will be left standing on the outside, in the dark.

2 Corinthians agrees, it reads: *For he says, "In the time of my favor I heard you, and in the day of salvation I helped you."*

I tell you, now is the time of God's favor, <u>now is the day of salvation.</u>[56]

Verses 11 & 12: *Later the others (foolish virgins*[57]*) also came. 'Sir! Sir!' they said. 'Open the door for us!'*

But he replied, 'I tell you the truth, I don't know you.'

The Bridegroom did not know those foolish virgins. They dressed, looked and spoke like their wise counterparts, but they were phonies. Truth, Grace, and the Holy Spirit that comes in with Salvation did not fill their hearts. They were empty of the <u>necessary</u> ingredients for entrance <u>with</u> the Bridegroom. But their hearts were not <u>totally</u> empty; they were full of unrighteous things; full of self-assurance, instead of God's assurance, full of self-righteousness, instead of His righteousness. They were also full of backbiting and complaining and apathy toward the bridegroom instead of Love, Peace and Joy in the Holy Ghost.

These foolish virgins sought to fill their hearts with His truth much too late, so they were not allowed to enter into the Wedding feast. The Bridegroom saw right through their façade, He could look straight into their hearts. He <u>saw</u> the emptiness deep within them. They appeared to Him much like Esau of old who came seeking the blessing of his father much too late. Who asked of Israel, while in a fit of crocodile tears, *"Haven't you reserved any blessing for me?"* Genesis 27:36b.

Jesus answered the foolish virgins correctly when He said, 'I tell you the truth, I don't know you.'

---

[56] 2 Corinthians 6:2
[57] Words in parenthesis added for clarity.

Jesus repeated this denial in Luke 13:24-28:

Make every effort to enter through the narrow door (strait gate[58]), because many, I tell you, will try to enter and will not be able to. Once the owner of the house gets up and closes the door, you will stand outside knocking and pleading, 'Sir, open the door for us.'

But he will answer, 'I don't know you or where you come from.'

Then you will say, 'We ate and drank with you, and you taught in our streets.'

But he will reply, 'I don't know you or where you come from. Away from me, all you evildoers!'

However Jesus did give us a warning at the end of this parable.

Verse 13, *Watch therefore, for ye know neither the day nor the hour wherein the Son of man cometh.* **KJV**

Jesus warned His listeners, as well as all those of who came after, to be ever watchful for His return. He has told us in Mark 13:32-33: *No one knows about that day or hour, not even the angels in heaven, nor the Son, but only the Father. Be on guard! Be alert! You do not know when that time will come ...*

This warning is for ALL who would hear His voice and listen to His call.

Proverbs also gives us a warning of our sleepy nature, *How long will you lie there, you sluggard? When will you get up from your sleep? <u>A little sleep, a little slumber,</u> a little folding of the hands to rest— <u>and poverty will come on you like a bandit</u> and scarcity like an armed man.* [59]

---

[58] Ibid. Found in KJV.
[59] Proverbs 6:9-11

The poverty Solomon was speaking of was the poverty of one's soul. If we remain in our slumber we can fall into the deep sleep of apathy to our Bridegroom. But there is still time to wake up and prepare for His return. And He is anxious for each of us to do so!

Song of Solomon 5:2, *I slept but my heart was awake. Listen! My lover is knocking:*

"Open to me, my sister, my darling, my dove, my flawless one. My head is drenched with dew, my hair with the dampness of the night."

The Beloved [Solomon] was calling to wake His flawless bride [the Shunamite woman][60] from her slumber so that they could spend time together. This is an example of Jesus – our Bridegroom – calling us to waken us from our slumber so that we are prepared for the wedding feast.

Ephesians 5:14b-15, encourages us to awake from our sleep and prepare to meet Him, ... *This is why it is said: Wake up, O sleeper, rise from the dead, and Christ will shine on you.*

There is still time for today's foolish virgins to become wise. Hebrews says; *as has just been said: Today, if you hear his voice, do not harden your hearts as you did in the rebellion.*[61]

The book of Matthew tells us: *But seek first his kingdom and his righteousness, and all these things will be given to you as well.*[62]

Seek to find His truth, Seek to have your heart filled to overflowing with His Salvation, His Grace, His righteousness, peace and joy in the Holy Spirit. When you seek Him with your whole heart, He is glad to reward you accordingly. As it says in Ephesians 3:16-19, *I pray that out of his glorious riches he may strengthen you with power through his Spirit in your inner being,*

---

[60] Words in parentheses added for clarity.
[61] Hebrews 3:15
[62] Matthew 6:33

so that Christ may dwell in your hearts through faith. And I pray that you, being rooted and established in love, may have power, together with all the saints, to grasp how wide and long and high and deep is the love of Christ, and to know this love that surpasses knowledge—that you may be filled to the measure of all the fullness of God.

Matthew 5:14-16 says; *You are the light of the world. A city on a hill cannot be hidden. Neither do people light a lamp and put it under a bowl. Instead they put it on its stand, and it gives light to everyone in the house. In the same way, let your light shine before men, that they may see your good deeds and praise your Father in heaven.*

We, as wise virgins and members of Christ's Bride, are to hold high our lamps to shine forth to the world and lead them into the body of Christ. So, let your hearts be full to over flowing with all that He has to offer you and shine your light in the darkness to draw foolish virgins and unbelievers to Him.

But do not forget this one thing, dear friends: With the Lord a day is like a thousand years, and a thousand years are like a day. The Lord is not slow in keeping his promise, as some understand slowness. He is patient with you, not wanting anyone to perish, but everyone to come to repentance. But the day of the Lord will come like a thief. The heavens will disappear with a roar; the elements will be destroyed by fire, and the earth and everything in it will be laid bare.[63]

Now that we have learned our lessons from the wise and the foolish virgins we can use them to be prepared ready to meet our Bridegroom. When prepared we can to return to the road that leads to our Marriage Supper with Jesus.

Are you ready?

---

[63] 2 Peter 3:8-10

Return of the Bridegroom
Step Ten

When all was prepared for his bride and the groom's father had given his approval, the bridegroom would gather his friends. They would all go in procession – much like a parade through the village – to the home of the Bride's father. When they were getting closer a groom's man would sound the Shofar – a horn made from the horn of a ram – and shout that the bridegroom was approaching to gather his bride. This had a dual effect; people of that village who heard the announcement would also join the throng, for all were invited to attend the festivities. Can we say ancient wedding crashers? Just kidding. The Father of the groom would be glad to have all who would enter. In fact families looked forward to the weddings of their village daughters. They were celebrated in Royal fashion, or as close to that as a family could afford. The announcement by horn and shout would also bring the Bride, dressed in her finest dress with her new veil covering her face, to attention. The bride's attendants gathered with her, lamps trimmed and ready, waiting to escort the happy couple to the wedding feast.

Joseph Returns For Mary

It has been about 18 months since Joseph was last seen at the home of Heli and his family. Mary, her sisters and friends are gathered in the living quarters of Heli, her father. They had been there for several days waiting for Joseph's return and the feast that would begin when their marriage was consummated.

It is about two in the morning when off in the distance a ram's horn is blown and someone is shouting. The sounds are too far away for her to be sure, but Mary is now awake. Gently she rouses her sisters and friends – the same ladies that were with her at the mikvah.

"Ladies," Mary whispers, "I think I have heard the Shofar. Joseph is on the way."

Mary and her attendants go to their lamps, blow them out, trim the wicks, fill them with oil and re-light them.

Again the Shofar sounds and the groom's men shout, "Awake, the bridegroom comes. Make ready his lovely bride." They are closer than before, but still a distance away.

The group of groom's men and villagers is growing, house by house, as they walk through Nazareth. They all surround a chaise where the groom is waiting for his bride. On their way through the village they wind through every street and avenue to make sure that all in Nazareth are given the chance to attend the wedding feast. Finally the entourage is just a couple blocks from Heli's house. Once more the shofar sounds and Joseph's men announce his coming for his bride.

"Make way the bridegroom is coming," the men repeat. "Prepare the way for Joseph. He comes for his bride."

The bride's maids surrounded Mary. They straightened her veil, and then checked their lamps one last time to be sure all was in readiness for the groom. Once all was prepared the group moved as one toward the doorway.

The shofar sounds one last time as the group stops in front of the home of Heli and his family. The entourage splits and the groom's best friend heads to the front door of the house. Quietly he opens the door and sweeps Mary off her feet in one swift motion. The bride's maids quickly fall in behind him and follow him back to the large entourage outside the family's fence. He hands Mary up into the chaise to Joseph, her bridegroom. Then the procession make their way back through the village to the home of Jacob, the groom's father and the wedding feast to come.

Christ Is Returning For His Bride

We, as Christ's Bride will also hear the sound of the Shofar – trumpet - and the announcement of His attendants – all the holy angels.

For this we say unto you by the word of the Lord, that we which are alive and remain unto the coming of the Lord shall not prevent them which are asleep. For the Lord himself shall descend from heaven with a shout, with the voice of the archangel, and with the trump of God: and the dead in Christ shall rise first: Then we which are alive and remain shall be caught up together with them in the clouds, to meet the Lord in the air: and so shall we ever be with the Lord. 1Thesessalonians 4:15-17.

And again in I Corinthians 15:51-53; *Behold, I shew you a mystery; we shall not all sleep, but we shall all be changed, in a moment, in the twinkling of an eye, at the last trump: for the trumpet shall sound, and the dead shall be raised incorruptible, and we shall be changed. For this corruptible must put on incorruption, and this mortal must put on immortality.*

As unexpected as a thief in the night, our Bridegroom will call us to arise and meet Him in the air. We will hear a shout and the sound of the shofar. It will happen quickly. We must be ready.

Matthew 24:27 says; *For as the lightning comes from the East and flashes to the West, so also will the coming of the Son of Man be.*

The Huppah
Step Eleven

The second half of the ancient Jewish wedding ceremony, or huppah, is also called the "home taking." The original meaning of the huppah was "room" or "covering." Legend has it that the very first Huppah was the wings of the angels as God presented Adam's wife to him. This picture has a ring of truth to it when you think of the description of the Mercy Seat that covered the Ark of the Covenant God had built in Exodus as His dwelling place on earth among men. It had two cherubim on top of it, facing each other with their wing tips touching. This ark held the marriage contract of the Old Covenant. So the cherubim on it's top as their huppah is a great symbol of the meeting place of God and men under the marriage canopy.

The huppah of ancient times was a special room built in the bridegroom's father's home. The bridal canopy eventually replaced this special room. The huppah [canopy] symbolizes the new home to which the bridegroom would take his bride.

In ancient days the bride and bridegroom were escorted to the bridal chamber where they would be alone for seven days while everyone else was feasting in the home of the bridegroom's father. The feasting would not begin until the marriage had been consummated and the proof [the blood stained sheets from the marriage bed] was given to the bride's father.

Isaiah 26:20-21 tells us of this time: *Come my people, enter our chambers and shut the door behind you, hide yourself as it were, for a little moment until the indignation is past. For behold the Lord comes out of His place to punish the inhabitants of the earth for their iniquity.*

Joseph and Mary Enter their bridal chamber
The wedding party has arrived at the home of Joseph's father. The villagers head into the living quarters of Jacob and his family, while the groom's men and bridesmaids escort Joseph and Mary to the bridal suite for their week of seclusion. Isaac, Joseph's chief friend, stations himself near the door and waits while everyone else goes in to party to wait for the feast to begin in earnest.

Joseph and Mary, grateful to finally be alone, embrace in a long deep hug. Very few words are spoken as they share their first kisses. The night fades into morning, and at the rising of the sun Joseph slips the sheets quietly out the door to the waiting Isaac … the feasting can now begin.

The Church Will Share The Huppah With Jesus

The spiritual parallel of the huppah for the bride of Christ begins as we are lifted up off the earth to be taken to our heavenly wedding chamber where we will spend our 'bridal week' with Jesus, our Bridegroom and King. I believe our huppah is much like the one described in the beginning of this chapter. The wings of the angels, the very same wings that covered Adam and Eve, will cover the Second Adam – Christ – and His Bride – the church. I believe it will be a spiritual representation of the Mercy Seat that covered the Ark of the Covenant:

> *Make an atonement cover of pure gold—two and a half cubits long and a cubit and a half wide. And make two cherubim out of hammered gold at the ends of the cover. Make one cherub on one end and the second cherub on the other; make the cherubim of one piece with the cover, at the two ends. The cherubim are to have their wings spread upward, overshadowing the cover with them. The cherubim are to face each other, looking toward the cover. Place the cover on top of the ark and put in the ark the Testimony, which I will give you. There, above the cover between the two cherubim that are over the ark of the Testimony, I will meet with you and give you all my commands for the Israelites.*[64]

For the Lord himself will come down from heaven, with a loud command, with the voice of the archangel and with the trumpet call of God, and the dead in Christ will rise first. After that, we who are still alive and are left will be caught up together with them in the clouds to meet the Lord in the air. And so we will be with the Lord forever. I Thessalonians 4:16-17

When we have joined Jesus in our bridal chamber the Marriage Supper of the Lamb will begin.

---

[64] Exodus 25:17-22

The Final Step - The Marriage Supper
Step Twelve

Following the seven days in the huppah, or bridal chamber, the bride and bridegroom joined their guests for a joyous marriage feast with singing, dancing, music and much merriment. Jewish weddings in ancient times were not considered complete until they were consummated. This was the very reason for the couple's seclusion.

The bride and groom entered into the newly prepared marital habitat to begin their married life. They would spend a week in seclusion while their whole village celebrated in the home of the bridegroom's father. But the celebration didn't start the minute the group arrived. There wasn't a reason for celebration yet. The party could not begin in earnest until the marriage had been consummated, and thus the Marriage Contract had been fully initiated. And legend has said that in the consummation of the Ketubah new life had begun - not just in the couple, but also in the womb of the bride. And many times this was the fact.

Outside the door a trusted friend [the fore runner of today's best man] or faithful servant would wait until the groom handed out the proof of the consummation of the marriage – the sheets of the marriage bed with the spots of blood spilt by the bride. These sheets with their blood and semen stains were proof of the purity of the bride and that the marriage had indeed been consummated. And now the party can begin!

Jacob Invites His guests To The Feast
Isaac quietly hands the marital sheets to Heli, who puts them into a bag to take home. Heli then approaches Jacob, Joseph's father, to let him know that the marriage had been consummated. They spoke together quietly for just a moment, then Jacob gathers the guests together;

"Friends and neighbors, the table is set and the feast is laid." Jacob announces. "Come into the banquet hall and join in the festivities."

Jacob's servants stood at the door to the banquet handing the guests beautiful garments to wear to the wedding feast. All who entered were covered in robes, like those of Kings and priests. When clothed correctly, they entered in to eat and drink. The drinking brought on great merrymaking, complete with singing and dancing.

The Marriage Supper Of The Lamb

In the ancient Jewish wedding the bride shed blood to prove her virginity. This is a natural occurrence for all virgins when they have intercourse for the very first time. Scientifically speaking – when she is penetrated the hymen breaks and issues a small amount of blood.

For the Church, Christ shed His blood on the cross to cover us with His purity. He was pierced in his hands, feet and side. His blood gushed forth to wash away our sin. Jesus imparts His purity and righteousness to each and every one who has given their lives over to Him as Savior and Lord. Before we come to Jesus we are filthy and so are any acts we do, even those that look righteous. Isaiah 64:5-7:

You come to the help of those who gladly do right, who remember your ways. But when we continued to sin against them, you were angry. How then can we be saved? All of us have become like one who is unclean, and all our righteous acts are like filthy rags; we all shrivel up like a leaf, and like the wind our sins sweep us away. No one calls on your name or strives to lay hold of you; for you have hidden your face from us and made us waste away because of our sins.

In Acts, Peter and John stood in front of the Sanhedrin. Peter told them where Salvation comes from:

> *Then Peter, filled with the Holy Spirit, said to them: Rulers and elders of the people! If we are being called to account today for an act of kindness shown to a cripple and are asked how he was healed, then know this, you and all the people of Israel: <u>It is by the name of Jesus Christ of Nazareth</u>, whom you crucified but whom God raised from the dead, that this man stands before you healed. He is 'the stone you builders rejected, which has become the capstone.' <u>Salvation is found in no one else</u>, for there is no other name under heaven given to men by which we must be saved.*[65]

---

[65] Acts 2:14-21

In Romans 1:16-17 Paul said, *I am not ashamed of the gospel, because it is the power of God for the salvation of everyone who believes: first for the Jew, then for the Gentile. For in the gospel a righteousness from God is revealed, a righteousness that is by faith from first to last, just as it is written: "The righteous will live by faith."*

> **Revelation 19:6-9:** *Then I heard what sounded like a great multitude, like the roar of rushing waters and like loud peals of thunder, shouting:*
> *"Hallelujah! For our Lord God Almighty reigns. Let us rejoice and be glad and give him glory!*
>
> *For the wedding of the Lamb has come, and his bride has made herself ready. Fine linen, bright and clean, was given her to wear."* <u>*(Fine linen stands for the righteous acts of the saints.)*</u>
>
> *Then the angel said to me, "Write: 'Blessed are those who are invited to the wedding supper of the Lamb!' And he added, "These are the true words of God."*

Jesus covers us with His righteousness at Salvation. We wear it just like the wedding guests wore the beautiful garments when they entered the wedding feast. This is why Revelation states that the bride is clothed in fine white linen. We are clothed in Christ; His holy purity is our wedding robe. All who have been washed in His blood have been declared holy – just as if we had NEVER sinned. To God, we look just like Jesus, inside and out!

Like the ancient Jewish wedding, when we enter in wearing our 'wedding clothes' there will be shouts of joy, songs of praise and dancing (yes, dancing), how exciting it will be! The Bride will dance for joy with her Bridegroom, King Jesus. She will sing praises to His name forever.

Those of us looking forward to the marriage supper of the Lamb must go out to the highways and byways and extend an invitation to others to come.

Go out quickly into the streets and alleys of the town and bring in the poor, the crippled, the blind and the lame.'

'Sir,' the servant said, 'what you ordered has been done, but there is still room.'

Then the master told his servant, 'Go out to the roads and country lanes and make them come in, so that my house will be full. [66]

When all have been gathered into the Kingdom of God that would come in, Christ and all of the heavenly hosts will come to earth and escort His bride – the church – into our spiritual huppah and into the Marriage Supper of The Lamb, just as we read in the Revelation 19 passage above.

Revelation 2:17: *And the spirit and the bride say Come! And let him who hears say, Come! And let him who thirsts, Come; and whoever desires, let him take the water of life freely.*

Revelation 22:20: *Surely I am coming quickly.' Even so, Come Lord Jesus, Come!*

BEHOLD, HE COMES!

---

[66] Luke 14:21b-23

In Conclusion

After reading through the scripture we can see that the church is indeed the Bride of Christ. And as such, she is a true and proper Jewish bride. But we cannot, <u>we must not</u>, forget that He has brought us from some very improper beginnings.

We need to reach out to others around us who are in the same places and circumstances we once were in and lead them through the Word into the household of faith so that they, too, can be a part of His Bride.

Let us not be like those who were invited to the feast and did not go when they were called:

> *Jesus replied: A certain man was preparing a great banquet and invited many guests. At the time of the banquet he sent his servant to tell those who had been invited, 'Come, for everything is now ready.'*
>
> *But they all alike began to make excuses. The first said, 'I have just bought a field, and I must go and see it. Please excuse me.'*
>
> *Another said, 'I have just bought five yoke of oxen, and I'm on my way to try them out. Please excuse me.'*
>
> *Still another said, 'I just got married, so I can't come.'*
>
> *The servant came back and reported this to his master. Then the owner of the house became angry and ordered his servant, 'Go out quickly into the streets and alleys of the town and bring in the poor, the crippled, the blind and the lame.'*
>
> *'Sir,' the servant said, 'what you ordered has been done, but there is still room.'*

> *Then the master told his servant, 'Go out to the roads and country lanes and make them come in, so that my house will be full. I tell you, not one of those men who were invited will get a taste of my banquet.'"*[67]

May we answer the call of Jesus wherever it may take us so that we can lead many to His feast when He announces the Marriage Supper of the Lamb!

---

[67] Luke 14:16-24

Kissed By The Beloved

Have you been held by the Beloved?
Caressed lovingly by His hands?
Wrapped up in the love He offers?
Held close and listening for His commands?
Jesus longs to closely hold you
Longs to caress you with His love
To share with you His deepest secrets
All the things for you He's planned

Have you been betrothed to the Beloved?
Waiting for your union to be complete?
Are you listening for His closeness?
Sitting daily at His feet?
Jesus longs for you to join Him
Wants you as His loving Bride
Seeks to seat you at His table
In the place of Honor, by His side

Have you been kissed by the Beloved?
Joined in oneness, wed to Him?
Have you left behind all darkness?
And your former life of sin?
Jesus longs to kiss you deeply
Waits to see you long the same
See Him standing in the pathway
He longs to take all guilt and pain

Were are you, oh bride of Jesus?
Are you longing to know more of Him?
Have you shunned all the world's dainties?
For the Best of Heaven to win?
Put aside your former lifestyle
Leave all of the past behind
Seek the kisses of the Beloved
Seek His very heart to find

I've been kissed by the Beloved
Been held close and felt His breath
But I've wandered far from His side
And felt again the strains of death
I'm now running to find my Beloved
Longing His caresses again to feel
To know again His Holy kisses
To be in the very center of His will

Never again alone will I wander
For my place is at His side
I've learned that the greatest honor
Is to be His heavenly Bride
Beloved I am drawing closer
Coming again to seek Your face
Longing to be held by Your caresses
Waiting to be kissed and in Your embrace

Other Titles by Leigh
Available at: http://www.lulu.com/spotlight/leighm

- **Praise: Through Poetry, Prayers and Prose**
  2nd Edition

- **Penelope's Perils**

- **Poetry of Christmas**

- **Serving In Singleness**

Seeking and Finding God's Best For Your Life

- **Having A Harley Christmas**

- **The Church: A Proper Jewish Bride**

Available at: http://www.lulu.com/spotlight/leighlea

- **Praise: Through Poetry, Prayers and Prose**

- **Mom & Dad, Fifty Years Together**
  A Tribute to Success

All Titles Available in Paperback and Ebook Formats

Other Endeavors by Leigh:

Freelance Writing at:
www.LeighsLetters.com
Leigh.mortons@gmail.com

Doula Services at:
http://lovingheartnhelpinghands.blogspot.com/
Leigh.lovingheartnhelpinghands@gmail.com

www.ingramcontent.com/pod-product-compliance
Lightning Source LLC
Chambersburg PA
CBHW031407040426
42444CB00005B/447